Missiology: a Study of the Spread of the Christian Faith

Copyright © 2004

All rights reserved. No part of this publication may be reproduced, stored in a retrieval system, or transmitted in any form or by any means, electronic, mechanical, photocopying, recording or otherwise, without prior permission by the author.

Published as a manuscript by
Kachere Series
P.O. Box 1037, Zomba, Malawi

ISBN 99908-76-07-X
Kachere Tools no. 2

Cover: Caroline Mkundi
Layout: Klaus Fiedler
Graphic design: Patrick Lichakala

Printed by Lightening Source

Missiology: a Study of the Spread of the Christian Faith

Timothy Nyasulu

Kachere Tools no. 2

Kachere Series
Zomba
2004

Series Editors' Preface

Since 1995 the Kachere Series has been publishing books as Kachere Monographs, Kachere Books and Kachere Texts, later being supplemented by Kachere Studies and Kachere Theses. All these books were designed for a general readership, and while we hoped that they would be useful for students and lecturers – a hope that has proven to be justified – none of them was written specifically for students. This title, the second in the new series Kachere Tools, is the first book specifically designed as a text book, as a book designed to accompany a specific course in an existing syllabus. We hope to be able to publish more such textbooks in the future. In addition we want to make public through this series any books that can serve as tools for learning, teaching and research. Therefore it is quite appropriate that the first book in this Kachere Tools series is the Polytechnic research directory.

Among the major theological disciplines, Missiology has not always had a firm place. But since the church in Africa is the result of missions, it is quite appropriate to devote time and effort to its study, not just as the history of the European and American missionary endeavours in Africa, but as a study of one of the crucial and defining marks of the church, be it in Africa or anywhere else.

This book, by Rev. Timothy Nyasulu, a lecturer at Zomba Theological College, has been written to match the Missiology syllabus (DT 23) of the Board for Theological Studies (formerly the Diploma Board) as approved by the University of Malawi. But we are convinced that even beyond its primary audience, the book may be of some use for all who learn or teach missiology, and for anyone who is interested in that subject.

Kachere Editors
February 2004

Contents

Chapter 1:	7
The Genesis and Development of the Mission of God	
Chapter 2:	11
History of Missiology as a Discipline	
Chapter 3:	17
Source and Biblical Foundation of Mission	
Chapter 4:	28
The Act of Mission: A Practical Application	
Chapter 5:	36
Motives for and Call to Mission	
Chapter 6:	41
World Wide Mission as seen from the African Perspective	
Chapter 7:	44
Major Periods of Christian Expansion	
Chapter 8:	61
Classical and Faith Missions	
Chapter 9:	72
New and Contemporary Approach to Mission	
Chapter 10:	87
Contextualizing a Congregation in Malawi	
Chapter 11.	93
Christianity and Islam	
Chapter 12:	100
Doing Mission and Fighting HIV/AIDS	
Chapter 13.	109
Co-Operation/Ecumenism and Unity in Mission	
Bibliography	

Preface

The 2003 academic year was uniquely interesting for me as a new lecturer at Zomba Theological College. Although it went contrary to my initial readiness, it was a blessing in disguise. My area of interest and specialization after attaining my MTh Degree at the University of Glasgow has been Biblical Studies-New Testament, particularly the study of Pauline theology.

When the allocation of subjects to each lecturer was done, I was given four subjects: Missiology, Practical Theology BD3, Preaching 2, and Old Testament 2. No New Testament? Anyway, I had to welcome and face a big challenge of preparing lessons for each subject.

Gradually, I liked the teaching profession and developed a special interest in Missiology. With the Help of Rev. Dr. D.S. Mwakanandi's (the former Principal of Zomba Theological College) Missiology workbook made for Theological Education by Extension in Malawi (TEEM) students, I found myself on the right truck. I should confess here, I mostly used his TEEM handout as my guide. A big 'thank you' to Baliska (Rev) Dr Mwakanandi for his notes. Graciously, Rev Dr. Stephen Paas also gave me his Missiology Course outline as he was to take the subject that year had I not come. This has also helped me greatly to create the subheadings of the project.

The 2003 second years ministers on training cannot go away without a pat on the back. They were just a wonderful class I always enjoyed interacting with during my lessons. Their critical constructive questions will always be remembered. The word 'MISSIO DEI' became part of their breath during Missiology periods.

Having all these stimulating tools, I was so pregnant that I finally decided to release what I taught in that academic year through this book. Thus the project focuses much on the Class lessons. I thank Dr Klaus Fiedler who encouraged me to compile my Missiology lesson material I have been teaching in 2003 so that it can be one of the Kachere Tools. I hope the book will benefit many readers especially scholars studying Missiology.

Timothy Kabulunga Nyasulu

Zomba, 2004

Chapter 1

The genesis and development of the mission of God

The original and authentic Christian tradition holds the view that 'all the generations of the earth' should embrace God's redemptive plan of salvation foreordained by God before the beginning of history.[1] In this case with no exception 'all generations of the earth' are the object of God's redemptive will and plan of salvation. Both in the Old Testament and the New Testament God has commanded his Church to communicate this message of his salvation to all mankind throughout the world. In the creation story after the fall there is mention of a seed crushing the head of the serpent (Gen 3:15). The popular interpretation is that the offspring (seed, Gen. 3:15a) refers to the coming of Jesus Christ whose coming (birth, life, death and resurrection) was solely and fundamentally to crush (defeat Gen 3:15b) the power of evil and death, which came with Devil (Satan).[2] The deluge to kill all creation except Noah and his family, who were saved by ark, was not just a historical event to put an end to all sinful people but was also a symbol of the recreation of the earth through the new ark- Christ.[3] Thus the calling of Noah to save the people from the flood was a commission with its own nature. In the Old Testament it explicitly starts with the call of Abraham in Gen 12:1ff. God promised that through Abraham he was going to bless all nations by establishing a covenant relationship. We see the descendants of Abraham called by God to fulfill his promise made to their forefather- Abraham. When Jews were in Captivity in Egypt God called and appointed Moses to liberate them from slavery and take them to the promised land, Canaan.[4] The election of the holy nation of Israel was that it was to be the light to the Gentiles and through it the whole world was to be saved. God called Moses

---

[1] Editors' introductory remark, 'What do we Mean by Missiology? *Missiology: An Ecumenical Introduction*, Grand Rapids, 1995, p. 3.
[2] Derek Kidner, *Genesis: Tyndale Old Testament Commentaries*, Leicester: Intervarsity Press, 1967, p. 71.
[3] David G. Burnett, *The Healing of the Nations*, Carlisle, Biblical Classics Library, 1996, p. 51.
[4] It is evident in the story of Abraham that the blessing was not restricted to the one whom it was promised. It overflowed to others. Paul calls Abraham the 'Father of Faith to all believers'.

in a burning bush, which did not burn up (Exodus 3:1-12). As the chosen people of God, although small as it was, Israel was never to be consumed by any earthly power so that the power and the glory of God would be manifested through her- Israel.[5]

In the wilderness God gave the Law (the 'Torah') to the Israelites through Moses at Mount Sinai (Read Exodus 19-32, Leviticus, Numbers and Deuteronomy) so that they could be guarded by it as they moved into the Promised Land, which symbolized the eventual birth of the Messiah. Although Moses did not himself enter the promised land, Joshua (The Book of Joshua) however, carried on Moses' mission and entered Canaan in. During the monarchy God was mostly interested in the keeping of the covenant relationship by observing the Mosaic Law. He urged kings, judges, prophets and priests to remember about what God did when he took them from the land of Egypt. Their deliverance from the bondage in Egypt was to remain with them as a remembrance and a point of reference about what God did to them to be transmitted to all generations to come. During the monarchy, when kings and priests failed to execute their duties, God appointed prophets to preach against unfaithfulness, idolatry, and injustice among his people. In some prophetic books there are prophecies about the coming of the Messiah who would come full of the spirit of wisdom and glory of the Lord whose delight would be in the fear of the Lord and who would judge with righteousness.

The Israelites' failure to obey the Mosaic Law which ended up breaking the covenant relationship resulted in punishment in exile. In exile God did not abandon his people. The message of hope was preached even in exile by Ezekiel (Ezekiel 1:1-3:1ff and 37:1-14). The prophets prior to Ezekiel like Isaiah, Micah and Jeremiah indeed had already prophesied about the coming of the Messiah who was to come to bring a new covenant. After exile, the Israelites resettled in their homeland, which was called Judah, and as Paul said (Romans 5:8) at the fullness of time the Messiah was born called Emanuel- God with us-and was named 'Jesus'- God saves (Matt 1:18-23).

Thus the story of the Old Testament on its own is a study of missionary movement. Its fulfillment is conspicuous in the New Testament when the Christian Church is born and established by the Holy Spirit. In the New Testament, which is the fulfillment of the Old Testament, the word proclaimed by Jesus Christ about the Kingdom of God is intended for all

---

[5] David G. Burnett, *The Healing of the Nations*, Carlisle, Biblical Classics, 1996, p. 48.

nations. Christ's birth, life, suffering and death had a missionary dimension. The Gospels are very clear that Jesus, sent by God, came to seek and save the lost people. The eyewitnesses were to share what they knew and had seen about Jesus Christ. After his resurrection, the message of resurrection was to be preached that 'Jesus is Lord.' In the Great Commission it is clearly noted that the apostles were to go and make disciples of all nations and teach them all what Jesus had commanded them. After receiving of the Holy Spirit at Pentecost (Acts 2) the disciples were empowered and went far beyond Jerusalem's frontiers preaching about the resurrection of Jesus Christ. Thus the nature of the Christian Church is missionary in the sense that it is a movement spreading the Christian faith, a body of persons sent to propagate evangelize.

In light of the above facts, we would define Missiology as the study of the foundation, the spread, and the growth of the Christian Church from the Old Testament up to the present day. Some scholars like Mwakanandi define Missiology as the study of the Christian Church in the world.[6] God has commanded his church in dependence on the Holy Spirit and by word and deed, to communicate the message of his salvation to all mankind throughout the world (Matt 28:16-20; Mk 16:14-18; Lk 24: 36-40; Jn 20:19-23; Acts 1:6-8). J. Verkuyl states "missiology is the study of salvation activities of God the Father, Son and Holy Spirit throughout the world geared toward bringing the kingdom of God into existence".[7] And it is very clear especially in the Acts of the Apostles that the early Church was passionately evangelistic as it disseminated its message so fast.

As the Christian Faith was spreading it reached people of different backgrounds. But to start with, Christianity started as a Jewish sect, which had broken away.[8] Consequently it faced a lot of resistance and persecution. The crossing of Christianity from Jerusalem to other parts of the world is closely associated with persecution.[9] The Church in Jerusalem was to a certain extent very Judaic. As it reached different soils the church germinated but

---

[6] D.S. Mwakanandi, *Missiology*: TEEM Notes, Zomba Theological College, p. 1.
[7] Johannes Verkuyl, *Contemporary Missiology. An Introduction*, Grand Rapids: Eerdmans, 1978, p. 5.
[8] James D.G. Dunn, *Jesus, Paul and the Law*, Westminster/John Knox, Kentucky, 1990, p. 131.
[9] Acts 8 and 9 give clear evidence that after the stoning of Stephen many Christians were scattered where they shared the Gospel.

with different environment it did not grow in the same way as it did in Jerusalem, even the areas of doctrinal emphasis differed.

The Church in Jerusalem with its typical Jewish background was not the same as the Churches in Antioch, Corinth, Ephesus, Galatia, which were Greco-Roman surroundings. For instance while in Jerusalem, James and some strict Jews emphasized the keeping of the law besides conversion, Paul in Galatia was more interested in grace, and in Corinth the manifestation of the gifts of the Holy Spirit was the burning issue in their services of worship.[10] From its inception therefore we can say that the Church has been diverse and dynamic in its missionary endeavours. It has never been static, more importantly it has sought its way and continues to seek its way in a diverse world of cultures, religions, socio-economic systems and political institutions. Influenced by these diversities churches today express their faith in a variety of ways: denominations have different forms of fellowships and theological reflection. But it must be underscored that such varieties should be treated as "Diversities in the expression of one Faith (Christian Faith)

---

[10] The dispute at Antioch between Peter and Paul (Galatians 2: 11-14) after the arrival of people from James (Jerusalem) indicates that the Church in Jerusalem was still legalistic compared to Antioch which was founded by Paul and Barnabas.

Chapter 2

History of missiology as a discipline

Although the study of mission dates from as old as the Old Testament story, the beginning of the Christian era and advance of practical mission work was given throughout the centuries of the church expansion, Mwakanandi reports that the first person to teach missiology systematically was the missionary to Muslims of North Africa towards the end of the middle ages, Roman Lull (1235-1315).[11] Other scholars who came later continued carrying out the work of missiology. According to Mwakanandi, the earliest Protestant training for mission was that of Anton Walagus in the Netherlands (1622). Voetius, also a Dutch scholar, was the first to develop a larger work on missiology in his book on church law (1663). It was, however, the German professor Gustav Warneck who published the first comprehensive missiology in five volumes, the first of those volumes in 1892. His work influenced all subsequent missiology.

The Term 'Missiology'

It has never been easy to find a suitable term for the theological discipline, which is now called Missiology. Scholars have actually debated a great deal to arrive at the term 'missiology', greater variety of names were proposed which include: Missions-Lehre - meaning theory of missions; Prosthetics- to add to the community (Acts 2: 41, 5:14; 11:24); Auzanics - to multiply and spread out; Halicutics - to fish for men. Other suggestions were 'Search', 'Theology of the Lost', 'Missionary Principles and Practice', 'Missionary Science', 'Theology of the Apostolate', 'Theology of Evangelism', etc. Eventually the name Missiology seemed suitable and became at least accepted internationally.[12] Looking closely at each definition, almost all the definitions had the element and notion of serving God by reaching out, but with a rich and wider spectrum. As a matter of fact, missiologists do not

---

[11] D.S. Mwakanandi, Missiology: TEEM Notes, Zomba, 2000, p. 3.
[12] Johannes Verkuyl, *Contemporary Missiology*, Eerdmans: Grand Rapids, 1978, pp. 1-2.

have problems that terms like spread, multiply, searching the lost and messengers are very crucial in missionary work.

Missiology as a Science/Study.

Missiology is a scientific discipline by its high standards of objectivity, historicity and critical understanding it applies.[13] It studies all the aspects of the mission of the Church. Mwakanandi comments further, as a science, missions of the church are critically and scientifically studied. "What it means here" Mwakanandi comments, "is that the same high standards of objectivity, historicity and critical understanding apply as in any other science. Many of the methods applied in human and literary sciences will be applicable in this field".[14] As a scientific discipline, the task of missiology is twofold, ie. normative and descriptive. In its normative function missiology provides norms and guidelines as to how the church has done and is doing its missionary work both in the past and in the present. It analyses, for example the motives, means and ways of mission work.[15] In its descriptive form it provides the historical facts, strategies and information about missions. By reflecting on what the church has been from its inception we can be able to see what elements contributed to its success and what elements failed. Our forging ahead depends on the past.

There is a wide variety of ways in which the church has carried out its missionary work and there are different concepts up to this day. Mwakanandi[16] records the following findings:

1. Mission was sometimes a special concern of an interested group of people.

2. Sometimes missions were a matter of spreading western civilization.

3. Sometimes mission was an associate of western expansion by subjection and colonization.

4. Sometimes it was undertaken by violent methods rather than by the spread of the word and loving service.

5. Sometimes the emphasis was on the planting of churches.

---

[13] *Reflection on Mission in the African Context,* edited by H.L. Pretorius, A.A. Odendaal, P.J. Robinson, and G. van der Merwe, Bloemfontein: Pro Christ Publications, 1997, p. 6.
[14] D.S. Mwakanandi, Missiology: TEEM Notes, p. 4.
[15] D.S. Mwakanandi, Missiology: TEEM Notes, p. 3.
[16] D.S. Mwakanandi, Missiology: TEEM Notes, p. 4.

6. Sometimes the expansion on the mission field took place as a result of heroic willingness to sacrifice.

7. Sometimes, every other religion was bitterly fought as demonic.[17]

What would be the comment from such approach to missions? Scientific study of missiology must offer a crucial evaluation of all these ways. And we must acknowledge that Missiology puts critical questions to mission and its theology. Therefore, scientific study of missions will reveal the glories of the church's mission, its weakness, its high points, its victories and defeats.[18] It is here that we find the concrete relationship between Missiology and Mission. Missiology is the science/study of mission. In studying mission we study the activities of the church.

Missiology as a Theological Study.

Missiology is in the first instance a theological science because it is fundamentally based on the work of God- MISSIO DEI. God the Father sent the Son into the world, the Father and the Son sent the Holy Spirit, the Son and the Spirit sent the Church to fulfill its calling as the visible body of Christ, continuing his witness and serving presence in the world. [19]

Missiology and other Theological Subjects.

J.H. Bavinck is reported in Verkuyl to have believed that missiology could be studied as an independent subject but it can never be isolated from other theological disciplines.[20] Thus agreeing with Bavinck we can easily say that Missiology as a theological subject works in close collaboration with all theological subjects. In its operation it is involved with all subjects.

A. *Missiology and Biblical Studies (Old Testament and New Testament).*

In Biblical Studies, especially in exegesis and hermeneutics,[21] missiology is supplied with both a good understanding of how the church ought to carry out its mission and a correct view of methods of communication. For example the book of Acts presents many models of gospel communication among

---

[17] D.S. Mwakanandi, Missiology: TEEM Notes, p. 4.
[18] Based on D.S. Mwakanandi, Missiology: TEEM Notes, p. 4.
[19] D.S. Mwakanandi, Missiology: TEEM Notes, p. 4.
[20] Johannes Verkuyl, *Contemporary Missiology*, p. 7.
[21] Johannes Verkuyl, *Contemporary Missiology*, p. 9.

various group of people of different levels. A proper understanding of such models is very important for missiology. [22]

B. Missiology and Systematic Theology and Ethics

Missiology relates itself to Systematic Theology in branches like ecclesiology. The study of the Church includes the study of its formation, organization, and growth and not forgetting the doctrines it believes and teaches. Ethics and missiology have a lot in common too. Ethics deals with ethical issues facing the Church.[23] Missiology derives a lot from Ethics. To be witness of Jesus means not only preaching the word, but also deeds- deeds of love, mercy, compassion and justice. These are basically ethical questions which missiology struggles with in its operation. As missiology has a bearing on ethical conditions,[24] it is indispensable to study missions together with ethical issues.

C. Missiology and Church History.

Missiology as the study of the mission of the church comes very close to church history.[25] Missiology has a lot to learn from history of missions. Therefore, Mwakanandi summarizes by saying, "the growth of the church across the world is mission history and also church history.[26]

D. Missiology and Practical Theology.

Missiology operates much like practical theology. The very least that can be said is that the two disciplines should work more closely together. The distinction to be made, perhaps, is that missiology specializes in the church in its outward orientation, while practical theology deals with the inner life of the church.

The Term 'Mission'

Mission is the primary source of missiology, which is the study of missions. Mission provides the material, which can be studied. Since the inception of

---

[22] D.S. Mwakanandi, *Missiology: TEEM Notes*, p. 5.
[23] Johannes Verkuyl, *Contemporary Missiology*, p. 10.
[24] D.S. Mwakanandi, *Missiology: TEEM Notes*, p. 5.
[25] Johannes Verkuyl, Contemporary Missiology, p. 10.
[26] D.S. Mwakanandi, *Missiology*: TEEM Notes, p. 5.

the Christian church in the New Testament, the following are some of the definitions of mission:

1. Mission is witnessing to the Kingdom of God. Jesus, the first and the prototype of all missionaries, come and said " the kingdom of God/Heaven is near. Later on he said the Kingdom of God is among you. And then in Acts 1:8 he told his disciples/followers "you will be my witnesses".

2. Mission is the propagation of salvation in Christ to those who do not believe in Him, calling them to repentance, conversion and faith in Jesus Christ. Those who respond and believe receive forgiveness of their sins and gift of salvation and are reconciled to God.

3. Mission is the conscious attempt to propagate the Christian faith among those who do not know Christ, or have lost their faith in Christ, or have no personal commitment Christ.

4. William Carey who is described as the Father of Missions (1792) states that mission is the use of all means for the conversion of the heathens.

5. Mission can also take place by means of almost unconscious influence exercised on others or by a spontaneous expansion.[27]

Modern Christian Usage of the Term Mission in Missiology

The Christian usage of the term mission only came into use from the 16th century onwards. Before that various terms were used, namely the propagation of the Christian faith (Propaganda Fidei), apostolic preaching (Praedicatio Apostolica), Preaching of the gospel to the whole world (Praedicatio Evangelii in Universio), etc.

Gradually all these concepts gave way to the term mission and the theological subject came to be known as the "Science of Missions or Missiology." But fact there was no complete unanimity in all ecclesiastical and theological circles as to what was to be understood by the term mission. Some people saw mission as the specific understanding of interested groups of Christians. Others saw it as the work of the church itself, for again others it was the secret driving force behind the expansion of western culture in the third world. For still others, mission was the umbrella term for everything God does in the world or for everything done by anyone for other people.

---

[27] D.S. Mwakanandi, *Missiology*: TEEM Notes, p. 5.

This latter idea led Steven Neil to observe on one occasion that: "if everything is mission, then nothing is mission".[28]

---

[28] D.S. Mwakanandi, *Missiology*: TEEM Notes, p. 6.

Chapter 3

Source and biblical foundation of mission

The Source of Mission

God himself is the beginning and continuation of mission. By his creation power, by the word together with the sending of the Son and Spirit God began mission. In this way God planted the church and gave it the commandment of mission. The source of all worldwide mission of the church is MISSIO DEI- the mission of God.[29] It is underscored by a number of writers that Augustine used the term Missio dei for the first time during the Trinitarian discussion. The term became current after the world missionary conference held in Willingen town in Germany to mean:

1. God's mission, not ours.
2. The missionary movement of which we are part has its source in the Triune God himself.
3. God engaging the Church as partner in his work.[30]

It has popularly been accepted that the Church by its very nature is missionary and that every Christian is essentially missionary. A Christian is sent out into the world as a witness for Christ and is in fact a co-worker with Christ. The commission has an appeal to the Christian life with its base on the Bible. Thus the mission has to be judged by the standards of truth to be found in the scriptures. But in the true sense, the mission begins with God. The mission activities displayed in both Old and New Testament show that God is the primary agent. He is the subject of mission, and the church at best is participating in God's mission. The initiative is not the church's or ours but God's. The mission of the church has no independent existence. "God is the chief actor in the drama of salvation, while people are merely bit players."[31] The chief aim of MISSIO DEI is salvation of his people in an inclusive sense. His Agape is the chief motive vindicated throughout the Bible.

---

[29] D.S. Mwakanandi, *Missiology:* TEEM Notes, p. 9.
[30] D.S. Mwakanandi, *Missiology*: TEEM Notes, p. 9.
[31] D.S. Mwakanandi, *Missiology*: TEEM Notes, p. 9.

The bible strongly accentuates God's love as motive for his mission and for the setting up of his church.

The Trinitarian Basis of Mission

MISSIO DEI is the mission of the triune God, i.e. God the Father, God the Son and God the Holy Spirit. Although one cannot precisely draw line how each person in the Triune God is involved, a general distinction can be made on the basis of scripture. It is clear from the Bible that the Father sends the Son (John 3:16), the Son sends his disciples and his church (Matthew 28:18-20; John 17:18), and the Holy spirit equips and guides the disciples (John 14:26; 16:13; Acts 2). Scott (1980, p. 99) observes that in the Old Testament the Father is of the greatest importance. In the gospels God the Son is pre-eminent, while the Holy Spirit is foremost in the Epistles. [32]

God the Father

God the Father is engaged in Mission work throughout the history of mankind. In the Bible we are presented in with a continuous series of God's messengers. Abraham is called from Ur to become the carrier of God's blessings to the nations. Moses was sent to be the agent of Israel's redemption. Old Testament prophets criticize the people of Israel because of failing to be faithful to the covenant relationship, which God created between the Israelites and himself. Because they failed to keep the covenant relationship and turned away to other gods, God himself would create a new covenant with Israel. This new covenant was going to be written on the hearts of people. In the New Testament, Jesus Christ is the anointed Son of God sent by the Father full of the Spirit to be the bearer of God's Kingdom.[33]

God the Son

In a certain sense Jesus takes over the mission from the Father. And he said, "as the Father has sent me, even so I send you" (Jn 20:21). During his ministry Jesus called disciples whom he could send as fishers of people (Mk 1:17). After he had accomplished his early ministry and before he ascended into heaven, Jesus sent his disciples into the world to do mission work. Jesus

---

[32] D.S. Mwakanandi, *Missiology*: TEEM Notes, p. 9.
[33] D.S. Mwakanandi, *Missiology*: TEEM Notes, p. 9.

continues to send his church on mission and as he promises it to be an 'ongoing church.'

God the Holy Spirit

The role of the Holy Spirit in the worldwide mission is vital. The Holy Spirit is the active agent of mission. Jesus had to make the disciples understand this right from the beginning; they were to be his witness in the world but not without the guidance of the Holy Spirit (Acts 2:8). When the Holy Spirit came on the day of Pentecost his power manifested immediately and abundantly in the experience of the evangelists. The witness for Christ in the world is carried out under the rule and guidance of the Holy Spirit. He equips the church always and goes before the church in her mission journeys. He changes people and opens the doors for the church's message. It can be concluded that only in dependence upon the Holy Spirit the church can do mission.[34]

The Church

An over emphasis on the divine task of mission poses a danger to the whole concept of mission because by so doing human responsibility disappears. Mission is not only God's task; it is also the task of the church. God provides for everything for his mission but the Church is there to implement. Jesus sends the Church (Jn 19:18; 20:21). The church in turn sends its members (Rom 10:15; Acts 13:13). Practically speaking, mission involves the whole life of the church. The church exists by mission. Mission is involved in both communicating and passing on the good news to those outside, and establishing and building up of churches. Thus as stated above everybody who claims to be a Christian is invited to this missionary work. It is not a one man's show. No one can deny that the Christian church is a missionary church. It is her very nature to be missionary. It exists by doing missions. It is the church 'on the way' or 'on the move'. This expression emphasises that the church can never be static and established, but must always on the 'go'. It is imperative that the church must be on the 'go'.[35] The church is a church only as along as it is missionary. The church's Christian message exists only

---

[34] D.S. Mwakanandi, *Missiology*: TEEM Notes, p. 10.
[35] W.R. Spindler, *The Biblical Grounding and the Orientation of Missions*, Grand Rapids, 1987,1995, p. 128.

in the form of being on the way to the peoples. A church without missionary work is like 'dead wood.' The church does not exist for its own sake but for the sake of the world for it is the world that God loves (John 3:16; Mat 28:18-20).

Doing mission is sharing what you have experienced and received from the Lord. The witness for Christ is bound up with the faith perspective. It has been noted by Blauw[36] and others that the aspects missionary dynamism is two-fold i.e. 'centripetal' and 'centrifugal.' The centripetal represents a drawing to the centre in the same way a magnet draws iron filings to itself. Here Blauw gives the example of Ruth and the Queen of Sheba, whereby both were impressed by Israel and were drawn to her. 'Centrifugal mission,' on the other hand, is flinging out into an active missionary task like with Jonah who was sent to go and preach to the people of the city of Nineveh in the Old Testament. However, when one arrives at the New Testament a new dimension emerges, and the commission is given to all peoples"(Spindler p. 53). Yes, indeed, the people are first attracted to the faith proclaimed by preachers or just the life of believers and become part of the group-centripetal-and then such people are compelled to share that experience with others and go to reach out-centrifugal. Such is how the ministry of the Christian church works.

We have clearly noticed that Missiology. It is not just a branch of theology; it is more importantly basing its authenticity and authority on the Bible. Thus the foundation of mission, whether Trinitarian or ecclesiastical, is the Word of God in the Bible. When we study missions we study what the church has done basing its truth on the Bible. Biblical studies, exegesis and hermeneutics Mwakanandi, supply missiology with both a good understanding of how the Church ought to carry out its mission and a correct view of methods of communication, also and how the message is to be applied.[37] For example as one studies the book of Acts one is presented with many models of gospel communication among various groups of people of different levels, which have been taken up as models of most present missionaries and churches. A proper understanding of such models is very important for missiology because they determine how mission has to be carried out.

---

[36] Johannes Blauw, *The Missionary Nature of the Church*, Lutterworth, London 1962, p. 34.
[37] D.S. Mwakanandi, Mission: TEEM Notes, p. 5.

Christianity is, at its very core, a missionary religion. As stated above, its foundation is the Bible. In the Old Testament God is described as the 'Sending God' and 'on the move' and in the New Testament Jesus is spoken of as the one sent from the Father (Jn 3:16) who also sends the Church on mission (Jn 20:12).

Old Testament Teaching on Mission

For many people it has been difficult to see the idea of mission in the Old Testament. If we look at the call of Israel by God himself, the message is about God wanting his chosen people to obey their God and keep the covenant. Probably Bowen's statement is nearly correct that "Israel's scripture seems to require the nation to belong to Yahweh alone, and to be separate from all people. If God had any message for the heathen nations, this message seemed to be one of judgement, not of salvation. In other words God's love for Israel seemed to be particular."[38] But a critical look at how God chose and sent his people, notes that certain texts have situations, which have both exclusive and inclusive conceptions. While it is correct that God chose his people exclusively for a purpose yet in some cases it repeatedly portrays God as the one who calls people and sends them to mission. For instance, Abraham is called the bearer of blessings for the nations (Gen 12:13). But before Abraham received the call there were other nations, which were not fundamentally different from Israel. Israel's beginnings and election were in real world history, which was born out of the call of Abraham.[39] Out of his own will and decision, God intended these nations (where Abraham belonged) to receive His blessings although these nations were worshipping the gods of their ancestors. Even today, many people tell their mythical stories about how their nations came into being and about their ancestral gods, but unlike other nations, Israel's beginning was in real world history in that through Abraham they knew the true God.

God patiently made a new beginning and from the ancient nations chose Abram by grace not just to receive his blessing but to carry it to others, not just to have the privilege but to have the responsibility. By calling Abraham God was exclusive in the sense that he followed Abraham's lineage. But by announcing that through Abraham all the nations will be blessed God was

---

[38] Roger Bowen. *So I send You*, SPCK, London, 1996, p. 16.
[39] David Burnett, *The Healing of the Nations*, p. 49.

being inclusive in his mission. "In you shall all the nations of the world be blessed". The missionary work that was given to Abraham was continued by his descendants like Isaac, Jacob and their lineage up to the coming of Jesus. We also see Moses is called and commissioned to deliver Israelites from bondage in Egypt (Ex 3:6-17).[40]

David, Burnett has carefully noted the main idea behind the election of Israel. For him, Israel's *bahar* (election) had two important connotations; the first is that of making a careful choice occasioned by actual deeds. Secondly, *bahar* implied a special purpose or mission. The election was not just a call to be kept to themselves but in the true sense a call to mission. Israel was to be God's witness among the nations. The prophets kept on reminding Israel that her election was not favouritism but a call to be God's people and to be the light to the nations so that God's salvation may reach to the ends of the earth (Isaiah 42:6) Jonah, an Israelite who in the first instance refused God's commission, was called and sent to be a missionary to the Gentiles of Nineveh (Jonah 1:1)[41] In exile Israelites were not to abandon their faith but continue to worship Yahweh even in a foreign land so that other people (Gentiles) could learn about the Living God of Israel.[42] The climax of God's mission is found in the birth of Jesus Christ, Emanuel, (Mulungu Alinafe) who came to save the world from sin (Matthew 1:18-23).

New Testament teaching on Missions

If we are to start with the mission of Jesus, we can say that Jesus himself at the outset did not have a universal mission programme. He so often limited his mission to the chosen Jews (Matthew 10:5; 15:24). He did not clearly prepare his disciples for a universal programme (Acts 10:14; 11:3; 15:1). As a matter of fact, his main teaching in the Gospels was the coming of the Kingdom of God first to the people of Israel.[43] But Jesus' revolutionary approach to most Jewish laws puts across a different picture altogether. His readiness to receive outcasts and sinners, which was contrary to Jewish law, symbolized that he came to save all people who had faith in him. For him, God was to reign in all the lives of people. His open declaration that he came to fulfill the law, his love for sinners, his love for outcasts, his teaching on

---

[40] David Burnett, *The Healing of the Nations*, p. 49.
[41] R. Bowen, *So I send You*, SPCK, London, 1996, p. 17.
[42] Roger Bowen, *.So I send You* , SPCK, London, p. 18.
[43] Roger Bowen, *.So I Send You*, SPCK, London , p. 26.

the unlimited forgiveness and reconciliation between God and people and between fellow human beings, his reinterpretation of the Law and his choice of the twelve disciples to create a new Israel are good and reliable sources that Jesus' concern was for everybody. The New Testament epistles to the Greco-Roman world are the interpretation of the life and work of Jesus. Therefore, from the beginning to the end, the New Testament is a missionary book. It owes its very existence to the missionary work of the early churches to the whole world. The Gospels are, as it were, living records of missionary preaching.

There are many references in the New Testament to Mission.

The Gospels

Matthew 24:14

"And this gospel of the Kingdom will be preached in the whole world as a testimony to all nations, and the end will come." It is very possible to think that the end will not come unless and until the Gospel is preached to all nations worldwide. According to this verse the missionaries will delay the coming of the Lord if the gospel has not reached everybody.

Matthew 26:13.

"I tell you the truth, wherever this gospel is preached throughout the world, what she has done will be told in memory of her."

Matthew 28:16-20

"Then the eleven disciples went to Galilee, to the mountain where Jesus had told them to go. When they saw him they worshipped him but some doubted. Then Jesus came to them and said, all authority in heaven and on earth has been given to me. Therefore go and make disciples of all nations, baptizing them in the name of the Father, and of the Son and of the Holy Spirit, and teach them to obey everything I have commanded you. And surely I am with you always to the end of the age."

According to the Gospel of Matthew, firstly, the end will only come depending on the fulfillment of the preaching to all the nations.[44] Secondly, what the woman did was not just the pouring of oil on Jesus' head but in doing so the act will be a testimony in memory of her throughout the world.

---

[44] Based on Hudson Taylor's idea on Faith Mission in Fiedler's *Story of Faith Missions*.

It is the woman's message, which will be preached to the whole world.[45] The mission work here breaks the human sexual and gender barriers.[46] Thirdly, for those carrying out the commission, it is the Triune God who is in charge of the Mission. The Christian Church is never left alone in carrying out the work of God. Fourthly, 'throughout' and 'the whole world', are key words to missionary work. There is no boundary and particularity of persons. Everybody must be reached with the Gospel. Fifthly, the authority of missionaries comes from Jesus Christ himself.[47] They have the power drawn from Jesus himself who is the head of the whole Christian community worldwide. "I will be with you to the end of the ages".

Mark 16:14-16

"Whoever believes and is baptized will be saved but who does not believe will be condemned. And these signs will accompany those who believe. In my name they speak in new tongues, they pick snakes with their hands, and when they drink poison, it will not harm them, they will place their hands on sick people and they will get well. After the Lord had spoken to them, he was taken up to heaven and sat at the right hand of God. Then the disciples went out and preached everywhere and the Lord worked with them and confirmed his word by signs that accompanied it." In Mark, firstly, salvation is only for those who believe.[48] Those who do not believe will be condemned because of their unbelief. Secondly, the saved are different from the unsaved by signs which accompany them as believers. Thirdly, Jesus left the mission in the hands of the apostles.

Luke 24:45-47

"Then he opened their minds so they could understand the scriptures. He told them 'this is what is written: the Christ will suffer and rise from the dead on the third day and repentance and forgiveness of sins will be preached in his name.' According to Luke, the power of resurrection was to convict people

---

[45] Based on Klaus Fiedler's class notes on 'The New Testament as a Missionary Book', TRS Chancellor College, 1996.
[46] Based on Women's Liberation Theology's (Feminist) idea of claiming equality.
[47] Burnett, *The Healing of the Nations*, p. 135.
[48] A step to repentance is to believe in Christ that he is the Saviour. The Christian teachings holds that salvation is for those who believe and repent of their sins and ask for forgiveness.

of their sins and grant forgiveness if they repent. The power of the gospel is in the death and resurrection of Jesus Christ.

The Acts of the Apostles

It has been unanimously agreed that the book of Acts is a missionary book. In Acts 1:8, Jesus said before his ascension, "And you will receive power when the Holy Spirit will come on you and you will be my witnesses in Jerusalem, and in Judea and in Samaria and to the end of the world. (Acts 2:5,8.) "Now there were staying in Jerusalem, God fearing Jews from every nation under heaven. When they heard the sound a crowd came together in bewilderment, because each heard them speaking in his own tongue." (Acts 8:1-5) "On that day a great persecution broke out against the Church of Jerusalem and all except the Apostles were scattered throughout Judea and Samaria. Godly men buried Stephen and mourned deeply for him. But Saul began to destroy the church going from house to house he dragged off men and women and put them to prison. Those who had been scattered preached the word wherever they were. Philip went down to a city in Samaria and proclaimed the Christ there "(Acts 11:19-21)." Now those who had been scattered by persecution in connection with Stephen travelled as far as Phoenicia, Cyprus, and Antioch, telling the message only to the Jews. Some of them however men from Cyprus went to Antioch and began to speak to Greeks also telling them the good news about the Lord Jesus Christ. The Lord's hand was with them and a great number of them believed and turned to the Lord" (Acts 13:1-3)." In the church at Antioch, there were Barnabas, Simeon called Niger, Lucius of Cyrene, Manaen (who had been brought up with Herod the Tetrarch) and Saul. While they were worshipping the Lord and fasting, the Holy Spirit said set apart for me Barnabas and Saul for the work to which I have called them.' After they had fasted and prayed they placed their hands on them and set them apart." Also Acts 17:22-31.[49]

Revelation 5:9-19

"And they sang a new song. You are worthy to take the scroll and to open its seals because you were slain and with your blood you purchased men for God from every tribe and language and people and nation. You have made them to be a kingdom and priests to serve God and they will reign on the

---

[49] New Community having been filled with the Holy Spirit went throughout the world to share the word of God.

earth." The primary purpose of the book of Revelation was not missionary. Probably it was meant to comfort the church in the situation of persecution. But the book nevertheless has remarkable missionary visions. Read also Rev 22:2.

We can conclude that the gospels were written to win people for Christ. This becomes very clear when we read the conclusion of the gospel of John (20:30-31) "Jesus did many other miraculous signs in the presence of his disciples which are not recorded in this book. But these were written that you may believe that Jesus is the Christ, the Son of God and that by believing you may have life in his name". The gospel of Matthew starts with the heathen coming to see the Saviour, and it ends with the great commission.[50] The gospel of Luke was written in a missionary situation (1:3-4). "It seemed good also to me to write orderly account for you most excellent Theophilus, so that you may know certainty of the things that you have been taught". Mark has no clear statement about the purpose of the book, but the climax of the gospel can be seen in 16:38 when Jesus died and the Roman heathen Centurion at the cross said, "Surely this was the son of God". The book of Acts describes the missionary expansion of the church. It is often said that Acts is the first church history. That is not wrong but it is much more than church history. The book of Acts is a missionary history. In addition to mission history the book contains a lot of missionary sermons (Peter's preaching in chapters 2 and 3; Stephen's preaching in 7; Paul's preaching in chapters 13:13ff and 17:22-31). In addition there is much inculturation in chapters 10 and 11 in which we read about Peter and the baptism of Cornelius.[51] Peter bases his decision to baptize Gentiles without demanding circumcision on the guidance of the Holy Spirit and does not follow what would have seemed to be good reason from scripture. This issue comes up again in chapter 15 at the Council of Jerusalem. The letters of the NT were written in missionary situations. The letters to Corinth for example reflect the problems of a young missionary church. Letters are the missionary correspondence of Paul.

---

[50] Klaus Fiedler, Missiology notes hand out, Chancellor College, TRS, 1996, p. 1.
[51] Based on Klaus Fiedler's idea of inculturation in the Book of Acts, Class notes and discussion, 1996.

Chapter 4

The act of mission: a practical application

So what really is 'Mission' from the above biblical references? The Bible, which is the revelation of God, has been identified as the source and standard of mission. The theological reflection pertaining to missionary activity has to be biblically founded and then passed on to those who are in need of it. M.R. Spindler has noted the meanings of mission in terms of obeying what Jesus expected the apostles to do. It is more to do with 'theology acted' rather than 'theology taught' or learned.

1. Mission is being sent out

"The pattern of 'being sent out' is the first biblical idea behind the concept and reality of mission. Jesus sent out the twelve apostles (Mat 10:16) and the seventy disciples (Lk 10:1). "Ask the Lord of the harvest to send out labourers into the harvest" ' (Mat 10:16) see also (Lk 10:2; Mat 9:38).' "As the Father has sent me, so I send you" (John 20:21). In itself the term apostle, like Isaiah in the Jewish tradition, stands for the one who is sent or the envoy, one who represents with authority the one who has sent. What is indicated therefore, is the distinct authority to represent Jesus and his Father in the power of the Holy Spirit.[52] Believers are simply messengers of God, the Father, Son and Holy Spirit.

Spindler[53] is very sure that it is Jesus who sent his apostles to do mission. They do mission in the name of Jesus. In the first place, mission is perpetuating what Jesus did. Jesus passes on the missionary task to believers. "As the Father has sent me so I sent you". Burnett with special interest in the occasion when Jesus said these words thinks that "seeing his nail-marked hands"[54] the apostles were impressed that the mission entailed suffering, and therefore so must theirs; however immediately Jesus goes on to give them the promise of the Holy Spirit. God sent him who accepted to suffer and he sends his followers who would equally suffer. Jesus transmits his authority

---

[52] M.R. Spindler, *The Biblical Grounding of Mission, in Missiology: an Ecumenical Introduction*, Grand Rapids, 1987, p. 127.
[53] M.R. Spindler, *The Biblical Grounding of Mission*, p. 128.
[54] David Burnett, *The Healing Of the Nations*, pp. 136-139.

to those who believed in Him. But possibly Burnett reminds us that those who accept the command should be aware of and ready for the consequences. Secondly, there is the issue of reinforcement. Indeed more workmanship is needed if his work has to be fulfilled successfully. God the Father and Jesus alone could not have done the mission to the whole world. But they thought of engaging his people to be co-workers with them. Thirdly, representation: a missionary is a representative as it happens with ambassadors in an embassy.[55] What makes their task distinct and unique is that they have the divine mandate, which is in the name of God the Father, the Son and the Holy Spirit, whom they represent. As an apostle the only thing to do is to obey the command of God. If one has been sent he does the work of the one who has sent him/her.

2. Mission is to make disciples of all nations.

Spindler says, "Mission is the universal and unrestricted opening of the new covenant. Acceptance of the new covenant necessarily implies an ethical obligation"[56]

The statement "make disciples of all nations" is in the first place an imperative. After all it is preceded by the commanding word "go". It connotes pedagogical action in the sense that you make disciples by teaching. Those who believe are to receive baptism- a rite that marks transition from 'old self' to 'new self.' There is transmission of both knowledge and wisdom. Secondly it has universal and ethical dimension in the sense that it applies to all nations. It has no particularity of any nation. All nations/people must be reached with the Gospel irrespective of cultural, racial, political and social background. The authority of discipleship is from Jesus. He is the one who charges his apostles. The actual task given by Jesus is "therefore go and make disciples of all nations." The Greek word μαθητευσατε[57] (make disciples) implies that the emphasis of the mission is to make disciples, of which baptizing and teaching and probably preaching too are necessary aspects. The verb "go" is placed at the beginning of both English and Greek sentences because it logically precedes the ultimate task of making disciples. In

---

[55] See the idea in Pauline Theology in 2 Corinthians 5: 11-20.
[56] M.R. Spindler, *The Biblical Grounding and Orientation of Missions*, p. 129.
[57] M.R. Spindler, *The Biblical Grounding and Orientation of Missions*, p. 128.

the making of disciples Christ is central and the disciple is placed under the authority of the master.[58]

3. Mission is deliverance, and emancipatory action[59]

As it is written in Luke, Jesus himself claimed that the Spirit of the Lord was upon him for the mission to the poor, the captives, the blind, and the proclaiming Lord's favour.

> "The Spirit of the Lord is upon me, because he has anointed me to bring good news to the poor. He has sent me to proclaim release to the captives and recovery of sight to the blind, to let the oppressed go free, to proclaim the year of the Lord."

4. Mission is a transforming service

The ministry of Jesus was holistic. He preached, taught and healed (Mat 9:35).[60] When he saw the hungry he was filled with compassion and gave them food (Mark 6:30ff).[61] Some people even followed him because they knew they were going to be fed (John 6:16ff). This is another important service that the Church is expected to do. These passages describe Jesus immersed among the people, ministering to their needs. Through teaching, preaching and healing Jesus reached and transformed people in all aspects of life, so we can conclude without doubt that Jesus mission was indeed holistic.[62] It would be advisable therefore, that those who are involved in fulfilling the great commission should not dare to separate the spiritual from the physical needs of today. John Stott comments,

> "It is not just that the Commission includes duty to teach converts everything Jesus had previously commanded (Matthew 28:20), and that social responsibility is among things which Jesus commanded. I now see more clearly that not only the consequences of the commission but the actual commission itself must be understood to include social as well as evangelistic responsibility, unless we are guilty of distorting the words of Jesus".[63]

---

[58] David Burnett, *The Healing of the Nations*, Paternoster Press, Carlisle, p. 137, .
[59] M.R. Spindler, *The Biblical Grounding and Orientation of Missions*, p. 120.
[60] Jesus' word to his disciples was that they should do the three-fold ministry.
[61] Cf the story of the feeding of the five thousand multitude.
[62] Escobar Samuel, *A Time for Mission*, Inter-Varsity Press, Leicester, p. 142.
[63] John Stott, *Christian Mission in the Modern World*, Inter-Varsity Press, Illinois, 1975, p. 23.

The gospel we preach today has the same impact on people and the Christian Mission is to be the agent of human and social transformation. Samuel Escobar argues that "Mission as service in Jesus' name involves proclamation of the gospel of salvation; life in fellowship in the body, which is the church; worship and prayer in Jesus' name as well as the multiplicity of tasks Jesus' disciples perform in response to human need."[64] Tasks are the services provided in terms of good deeds to others. We ought to be reminded at this point that mission is patterned on the example and saving death of Jesus who, in his own words, 'did not come to be served but to serve and to give his life as a ransom for many.

Thus today the church mission should consist of service both spiritual in proclamation of the word and of the physical in meeting human needs according to Jesus' model and in his name. It is so encouraging that many churches are involved in providing social services: establishing hospitals, schools, development projects, relief, Aids, or HIV/AIDS Programmes which look after the sick and orphans.[65] Since such services are fulfilling the holistic mission of Jesus, the already existing services should be intensified, but to those churches that have not started, why should they not start now?

The goal/purpose and models of mission.

To investigate the goal and purpose of mission work is an important search and great practical importance, for it determines missionary strategy and the choice of means and methods. In history the search has revealed various views as to *the goal and purpose of mission* some of which are listed below:

The goal of saving individuals.[66]

As already mentioned above missionary work is deliverance and liberating as recorded in Luke 4:18-19 some have emphasized the view that the task of mission is to save individual souls.[67] Jesus, though deeply touched by the multitudes, took a keen interest in individuals like Nicodemus, a Samaritan woman, a blind man along the way, a robber hanging next to him on the cross. Thus the genuine interest must be on saving individual souls. If, therefore, churches ever neglect the needs of the individuals as they seek to dis-

---

[64] Samuel Escobar, *A Time for Mission*, p. 153.
[65] The idea is based on Escobar's, *A Time for Mission*, p. 154.
[66] Johannes Verkuyl, *Contemporary Missiology*, Grand Rapids, 1987, p. 176.
[67] D.S. Mwakanandi, Missiology: TEEM Notes, p. 16.

charge their missionary calling, they in effect sabotage the commands of Jesus. Some of the advocates of such a goal include the early Pietists and William Carey (1761-1834).

The ecclesiocentric goal.[68]

Certain missionary movements have urged for the implanting of churches as the main goal of mission. Once planted, there has been also the emphasis of rooting the church with all its tradition and structures in the new societies. Such aims also appear as ecclesiastical goals in Roman Catholic teaching and also with the early reformers.[69] While such approach considers all the churches as belonging to one major church, the hierarchy in the Church can be a stumbling block to evangelism and mission.

The goal of church growth.

Verkuyl writes this goal is most important in the view of Donald McGavran in 1960[70] of the school of church growth in California in USA. According to him, as churches discharge their missionary calling, they must gear all their efforts to produce numerical church growth. Quantitative expansion is top priority of the churches' business.[71] Churches therefore should employ mass movements to multiply themselves. As Jesus commanded to go to the whole world to make disciples of all nations, it is imperative that the church should expand beyond its geographical borders. There is also an emphasis on the fellowship of believers. Those who have been made disciples are to come together to strengthen one another and then go to share what they have with others.

The goal of autonomous churches.

The two known exponents of this goal were Henry Venn (1724-1795) an Englishman and secretary of the Church Missionary Society, and Rufus Anderson (1706-1788), an American and secretary of the Board of Commissioners for Foreign Missions. During the 19th century, at about the same time, they began to articulate a goal for mission that called for building up

---

[68] Johannes Verkuyl, *Contemporary Missiology*, Grand Rapids, 1987, p. 181.
[69] D.S. Mwakanandi, Missiology: TEEM Notes, p. 16.
[70] Johannes Verkuyl, *Contemporary Missiology*, p. 189.
[71] D.S. Mwakanandi, Missiology: TEEM Notes, p. 16.

"self-governing, self-supporting and self-propagating churches" in short called "the three self formula."

Models of missions: methods and means of doing missionary work.

Escobar has summarized the history of Christian Missions as "the way in which people in thousands of cultures and languages have come to know Jesus, the way in which the name of Jesus has been honoured from country to country, from culture to culture, from language to language and from century to century."[72] People have experienced the presence of Jesus in their life with both spiritual and physical needs. Jesus, the best missionary,[73] and the pioneer of mission in the New Testament (John 3:16; Luke 19:10) saw his early mission as a three-fold task, the elements of which are complimentary and supplementary. These were preaching, teaching and rendering other forms of relevant services aimed at various needs like healing (Luke 4:18; Luke 4:23). This has been the task of the followers up to today. As such, in the history of mission work, in one way or another the church has followed this pattern since the apostolic age (see Acts 2:42; 3:1-10; 5:17; 8:4). Though each is related to the other as indicated above, distinction needs to be indicated as follows.

Preaching

Preaching was the first missionary way of conveying the Christian faith to the people who had never heard the Gospel. According to Burnett[74] in the gospels (Mark 16:15 and Luke 24:47) there are too words with the same meaning, firstly the Greek word κησυσσω translated "to preach," which refers to the proclamation of the gospel. Secondly, ευαγγελιξομαι be translated 'to evangelize,' which can also means 'to preach.' Both words can interchangeably be used to refer to the work of evangelism and have the central emphasis upon the work of witnessing to Christ as the saviour of humankind.[75] The Church today continues to spread the gospel. Of all the ways and means of evangelism, preaching seems to be the most common one taken by many missionaries whether foreign or local.

---

[72] Samuel Escobar, *A Time for Mission*, Inter Varsity Press, Leicester, 2003.
[73] Samuel Escobar, *A Time for Mission*, Inter Varsity Press, Leicester, 2003, p. 97.
[74] David Burnett, *The Healing of the Nations*, Paternoster, Carlisle, 1996, p. 137.
[75] D.S. Mwakanandi, *Missiology:* TEEM Notes, p. 17.

Theological teaching/education.[76]

Jesus Christ is regarded as the greatest of the renowned teachers in the history of the Bible and Christianity. Just from his youthful age up to the time when he called his disciples Jesus amazed many people in synagogues as well as in the streets. During the three years with his disciples Jesus was the greatest interpreter of the Mosaic Law. All apostles and the church fathers in history taught following the footsteps of their Master Jesus.

Therefore, just from the beginning the Christian Faith has not ignored Education. Education is seen as one of the important means to facilitate the spreading of the gospel of salvation.[77] Teaching people to read is to enable them to know God and Christ by reading his word. Education is also important as one way of training and equipping individuals to do missionary work among their own folks.

Bible translation and distribution.[78]

One of the biggest challenges to the spread of Christianity worldwide was how to pass the gospel to people of different language and culture. The early literature was mainly in Hebrew, then in Greek and latter in Latin.[79] This kind of situation was probably easier for places in the Middle East and some parts in the Roman Empire. It became difficult as the gospel crossed beyond these frontiers. Translating the Bible into the local languages was regarded as an important factor. Bible societies from an early date called for the translation of the Bible into the language of the people. Such translations have become a well-high indispensable help and blessing for missionary work. Similarly, the printing and distribution of Christian literature was regarded as important. Christianity was planted solidly in any given community.

Service/diakonia[80]

Jesus was a prophet mighty in both 'word' and 'deed' before God and all the people (Luke 24: 19). Service is mainly to do with deeds to meet the needs

---

[76] Johannes Verkuyl, *Contemporary Missiology*, Grand Rapids, 1987, p. 207.
[77] D.S. Mwakanandi, Missiology: TEEM Notes, p. 17.
[78] Johannes Verkuyl, *Contemporary Missiology*, Grand Rapids, 1987, p. 208.
[79] Johannes Verkuyl, *Contemporary Missiology*, Grand Rapids, 1987, p. 208.
[80] Johannes Verkuyl, *Contemporary Missiology*, Grand Rapids, 1987, p. 212.

of people you serve.[81] A true mission worker does not only address the spiritual and political needs of a person. For this reason missionaries rendered services aimed at various human needs. At the same time, such services were to evangelize. If we take healing services, for example, people who came to mission hospitals for treatment are also taught about God and his son, Jesus Christ.

Fellowship/koinonia[82]

Koinonia was one of the means used in introducing people to Christ. Jesus" incarnation among others was *koinonia*. He came to dwell among us. He participated with the people in their worrying, disappointments, joys and suffering. This caused people to see his glory and accept him (Jh 1:14; 14:9).

The majority of missionaries saw *koinonia* as one of the means par excellence of introducing people to Christ. Therefore today's churches must stimulate new ways of creating fellowship as a means of winning people to Christ. Those who are won are gathered into a fellowship community, which the Bible calls Ecclesia. This is important because no one can survive and thrive in the Christian faith all by himself. People need each other as together they journey the road to the Kingdom. For this reason *koinonia* is indispensable and ought to be encouraged at all costs.

Radio and Television[83]

These means have become increasingly valuable in modern times of high technology. Millions of people hear the word of God through radio and TV.

---

[81] D.S. Mwakanandi, Missiology: TEEM Notes, p. 18.
[82] Johannes Verkuyl, *Contemporary Missiology*, Grand Rapids, 1987, p. 221.
[83] Johannes Verkuyl, *Contemporary Missiology*, Grand Rapids, 1987, p. 209.

Chapter 5

Motives for and call to mission

We noticed in the above chapters that the source of all worldwide mission is God. That the motive of MISSIO DEI is basically to establish the Kingdom of God cannot be overemphasized. People of the earth should receive the will and the plan of salvation. Thus firstly missiologists have the interest of sharing the Christian faith. They deal with missiology basing on their faith in God the Father, the Son and the Holy Spirit. Secondly they have a theological interest, which is concerned with the whole world, "the ends of the earth". World in this case is human beings as in John 3:16, referring to all races. To this effect, the missionary task demolishes the walls of separation, it crosses the human frontiers, and it is for reconciliation. As it breaks the walls and advocates the reconciliation, it at the same time fights against principalities of the world. It is a mission fighting a war against the powers that aim to punish the world by losing the eternal plan of God.

However, although it is clear that the foundation of missions is God, the motives to carry out the mission are diverse. Some motives are pure and others are impure. Probably it would be important to mention that throughout the history of Christian Missions both pure and impure motives have been regarded as deep motives for communicating the Christian faith and have influenced the establishment of missions in different parts of the world. Verkuyl lists pure and impure motives respectively.[84]

(A) Pure Motives

1. The Motive of Obedience

The motive of obedience plays a very definite role throughout the missionary task. The missionary task is nothing more than obedience to the command of the Lord (Matthew 28:18-20).[85] The motive has inspired countless thousands to dedicate their lives to the missionary task. So if one gives up mission both at home and abroad he/she is being disobedient to his/her Lord.

---

[84] Johannes Verkuyl, *Contemporary Missiology*, Grand Rapids, 1987, pp. 164-173.
[85] This refers to the fulfilment of the Great Commission in Matthew 28:16-20.

He/she must hear once again the strong call to obedience. In the same way, today, churches on every continent need to be continually reminded of their need to obey the command of the Lord. It is in fact a challenge laid before the global church. It is not only a challenge to reach out, but also a challenge to live our lives with a missionary stance with a sense that one's presence has a purpose in God's plan for the world).[86] As people wander with the gospel to the unreached, they themselves are letters to be read by those who have not known Christ, as St Paul wrote to the Corinthians.

2. The motives of love, mercy and pity[87]

The Bible strongly emphasises the motives of love, mercy and pity in mission work. Jonah was accused of lacking these qualities when he tried to evade his missionary task to the Gentiles of Nineveh. In this motive, the missionary must have a concern for the lost, must be willing to share what he/she has experienced, he/she is passing on what he/she has been given by the Lord. Paul writes to the congregations that they have been rescued and now live by the love of God and must reflect that very same love to others through the work of mission. The objects of God's mercy and pity must now become the instruments and communicators of that mercy and pity to others. Christ wants to reach out to others via the congregation. But the church can only act as God's bridge to the world if she is filled with the same love, mercy and pity as he or herself has received from God.

3. The motive of doxology[88]

Praise to God's name is another of the motives for mission found throughout the New Testament. Paul says his concern is that "the word of the Lord may speed in triumph through the world and that every tongue confess that Jesus is Lord, to the glory of God the Father (1 Thess 3:1, Phil 2:11). Thus, one does mission as an act of appreciation, thanking God for what he has done and that the acceptance of Christ by people is for the sake of God's glory. It is a call that everyone, every tongue (including those who deny him now) must confess that Jesus is Lord. The motive of doxology has inspired the life of many missionaries who during the centuries have participated in the missionary enterprise. For Samuel Escobar, he thinks doxology is done by giv-

---

[86] Johannes Verkuyl, *Contemporary Missiology*, Grand Rapids, 1987, p. 164.
[87] Johannes Verkuyl, *Contemporary Missiology*, Grand Rapids, 1987, p. 165.
[88] Johannes Verkuyl, *Contemporary Missiology*, Grand Rapids, 1987, p. 165.

ing thanks to God for the mystery and glory of his gospel. "Jesus Christ" he says, "is the core of the gospel, which as a potent seed has given birth to innumerable plants," therefore is worth to be praised. It is moreover true that many men and women everywhere feel that he is their Saviour and Master who has released them from the bondage of sin and death.[89]

4. The eschatological motive[90]

It is not only the message of today. It is also the message for the coming time. When the Kingdom comes it is realized as well as eschatological. The motive of the Kingdom plays an important role in the gospels. The second petition of the Lord's Prayer, "thy kingdom come" expresses this central motive clearly. If one is in the Kingdom it is not only for today, it is also for the rest of one's life. Many missiologists note how important this motive was to the pioneer missionaries.

5. The motive of haste[91]

The motive of haste is closely tied to the motive expecting the Kingdom. Jesus was calm, yet at the same time he intensely hurried as he discharged his divine mandate in the cities and villages he visited. Paul too showed an inner security about his faith and yet was driven by deep compulsion to get the message out quickly. This motive presents to us the point that mission is a matter of urgency. The message should get the people as soon as possible, before the parousia, the second coming of the Lord.[92] Therefore, we must as Christians, be alert to what the New Testament calls the "times and seasons" and take appreciative advantages of them while it is still daylight, for the night is coming when no man can work.

---

[89] Mwakanandi, *Missiology*: TEEM Notes, p. 14.
[90] Johannes Verkuyl, *Contemporary Missiology*, Grand Rapids, 1987, p. 166.
[91] Johannes Verkuyl, *Contemporary Missiology*, Grand Rapids, 1987, p. 167.
[92] Mwakanandi, *Missiology*: TEEM Notes, p. 15.

B. Impure motives[93]

1. The Imperialist motive[94]

One of the frequent criticisms made of missionary work, particularly of missions originating in the west, is that it was done for imperialist reasons. By imperialism it means the attempts by one state to use another people as a means to achieve its own goals. Missionaries have often been accused of having been emissaries preparing the way for the occupation of new lands by colonizers.[95]

2. The cultural motive[96]

During the 19th century, the mission work went hand in hand with transfer of the missionary culture. For example some westerners believed that missionaries should go only to those areas where western culture had penetrated and seek to transmit and transfer to those people the deeper values of the culture. F.D. Schleiermacher, a theologian believed that mission work was primarily a cultural enterprise and he believed that mission work was accompanied by a general transfer of culture. Mission involves cultural extension.

3. The commercial motive[97]

Though the commercial motive never dominated, it often became an accessory motive and a point in the propaganda for mission. For example, David Livingstone wove genuine missionary motives with commercial interests. In 1856 Livingstone expressed in England his missionary aims as follows: "sending the gospel to the heathen...must include much more than this in the usual picture of the missionary, namely a man going with a bible under his arm. The promotion of commerce must be attended to move more speedily than anything else."[98]

---

[93] Johannes Verkuyl, *Contemporary Missiology*, Grand Rapids, 1987, p. 168.
[94] Johannes Verkuyl, *Contemporary Missiology*, Grand Rapids, 1987, p. 168.
[95] Mwakanandi, Missiology: TEEM Notes, p. 15.
[96] Johannes Verkuyl, *Contemporary Missiology*, Grand Rapids, 1987, p. 171.
[97] Johannes Verkuyl, *Contemporary Missiology*, Grand Rapids, p. 172.
[98] Taken from one of the London Missionary Society documents.

4. The motive of ecclesiastical colonialism[99]

This accusation of the western missions is greater in Africa and Asia. Ecclesiastical colonialism is the urge of missionaries to impose the model of the mother church on the local churches among whom they are working rather than give the people the freedom to share their own churches in response to the gospel. The western churches have often imposed their ecclesiastical structure on the churches in Africa and Asia. The result is that these churches look more like the western churches than the church in the New Testament.

---

[99] Johannes Verkuyl, *Contemporary Missiology*, Grand Rapids, 1987, p. 173.

Chapter 6

World wide mission as seen from the African perspective (a critique)

The popular notion is that a missionary must be a white person. For example two missionaries one black and another white. Usually only the white one will be regarded as a missionary among Africans. But don't they do the same work? It has been made to believe that a missionary must come from Europe, America or Australia.[100] But probably it is also important to know the meaning of a missionary. Mission and Evangelism, although they have often been used interchangeably, are not exactly the same. Doing missionary work basically means reaching the unreached with the Gospel. Evangelism has mainly to do with nurturing the already reached Christians. There is no demarcation as to who should do the work and to whom-any believer can do that to any person.

If we agree with the definition above, then definitely there must be something wrong with the assumption that missionaries are only from abroad particularly from the West. Probably before one starts giving the arguments that all can be missionaries to any place at any time, it would be interesting to give the brief Christian church background and its expansion. As a matter of fact Christianity has been in Africa nearly from its inception. Some scholars have recorded that Simon of Cyrene, who carried the cross of Jesus came from Africa. An Ethiopian Eunuch who went to Jerusalem to worship, although we are not told that he witnessed his experience of his trip and his baptism by Philip to other people, it is very possible that he might have shared with some people around his home area but was not recorded. These in the Bible play a significant role in witnessing to the life and death of Christ which subsequently contributes to the life of the Church. If we go far back' the Israelites lived in Egypt for many years from the time of Joseph who worked for Potiphar up to the time of Moses who delivered them from the bondage under Pharaoh leading them to the promised land Canaan.

In the New Testament, Joseph and Mary found refuge in Egypt when king Herod had decided to kill the baby Jesus. The Coptic church, which is still

---

[100] D.S Mwakanandi, Missiology: TEEM Notes, p. 7.

existing today, the Ethiopian Orthodox Church which had its roots from Frumentius and Aedesius, had their beginning in the first centuries of Christian history. Augustine, Tertullian and Cyprian[101] are among the first African theologians beginning with school of Alexandria in North Africa which has influenced Christian doctrines to a great deal. These are the bases that most Africans would strongly claim to have been evangelized earlier than most parts of the world. But probably Africans did not participate in mission work enough. Or the approach to missionary work was not like that brought by westerners. Or because of financial constraints and luck of facility Christianity did not go far. But to be sure Europe and America received Christianity at dates after Africa had already received it.

It has been observed by recent missiologists that the notion that a missionary must be white has come from the colonial phenomenon which came during the later centuries when Europe and America came to Africa for slave trade and gold in the west and later spread to the rest of the continent.[102] With this in mind it could be true that modern missionary movements originated in Europe and America to reach the unreached places. And indeed, Christianity of Africa-especially South of the Sahara owns its existence to these missionary movements. But even in those years of the early modern missionary movements not all missionaries were white. For example in Uganda, in most areas African evangelists were the first and were strongly supported by chief Kabaka. In Nigeria Christianity was very missionary and missionaries came from Sierra Leone. One of the famous missionaries was an African-Samuel Crowther who later became the bishop of Niger. In Malawi there were right from the beginning black missionaries from South Africa trained at Lovedale like Shadrack Ngunana, Isaac William Wauchope, Mapas Mtitili, Isaac William Ntsusane Koyi. William Koyi was the pioneer missionary to the Northern Ngoni.[103] He was very useful when he went to see Chikusi and Mbelwa chiefs to establish contact. In 1883 he started the pioneer missionary work among the Northern Ngoni. He died in 1886. Tom Bokito and Sam Sambani were Malawians whom David Livingstone had freed from the Arab slave traders in 1861 who had eventually been

---

[101] Stephen Paas, *A Conflict on Authority in the Early African Church*, Zomba, Malawi, 2000, pp. 10, 47-56.
[102] D.S Mwakanandi, *Missiology*: TEEM Notes, p. 7.
[103] John Weller and Jane Linden, *Mainstream Christianity to 1880 in Malawi, Zambia and Zimbabwe*. Mambo Press, Gweru, 1984, p. 43.

to Lovedale. They likewise helped mission work. Bokito in particular worked with Henry Henderson to begin the Blantyre mission in 1876.[104] And it is true that with all missionaries there was the teacher-evangelist missionary who did the greatest work in the evangelization of Africa. Peter Bolink a missionary to Zambia commented "it is highly doubtful whether the foundation of the church in central Africa could ever have been led by missionaries alone".[105] A big share of honour must go to those hundreds of Abrahams, Isaacs, Jacobs, Lukas and Mateyus who as teacher evangelists with little knowledge but often with great zeal to spread the good news to the remotest central Africa. Probably this is applicable not only to Central Africa but to the rest of Africa. When foreign missionaries came they did not know the places, language and culture. So they used Africans to do their missionary work. Unfortunately it is easily forgotten to remember that their missionary success depended on the local people they found.

In conclusion we can say that a Christian missionary can be anybody from any place at any particular time carrying the banner of bringing the good message to the unreached.

---

[104] D.S. Mwakanandi, *Missiology*: TEEM Notes, p. 7.
[105] D.S. Mwakanandi, *Missiology:* TEEM Notes, p. 7.

Chapter 7

Major periods of Christian expansion

This chapter is the longest of all chapters because it tries to cover both the historical and missiological events in a more detailed way.

The major periods of Christian expansion are mainly to do with the growth of the Christian Church since its inception. Growth is a sign of healthy life; be it to a plant, an animal, or a human being. However we need to be reminded that there are many factors that can hinder growth. Malnutrition, diseases, unfavourable environmental conditions and the like can be detrimental to the growth of any organism. The Church is no exception. From the time of its inception at Pentecost, the new community[106] of the Kingdom which came into being has survived a lot of challenges and obstacles up to this day. Praise God that the Church of God will never die.

An important missionary idea we need to be aware of on church expansion is 'the concept of growth'. Different people have referred to the growth of the church with different concepts. Some look at the numerical growth as spiritual growth. If the Church is growing in numbers people become glad that their church is growing. For example the Church in Africa grows much faster than the Church in Europe and America. Some have questioned as to whether growth in numbers can determine the growth of the Church spiritually. Nonetheless, anything which hinders the growth in any way is an enemy to the organism.

Jesus himself came teaching about the kingdom of God, and a major aspect of that teaching is that the Kingdom will grow. The agricultural motif of so many of the Kingdom parables such as that of the mustard seed and the yeast, leaves one in no doubt about the growth of the Kingdom. However Jesus made it equally clear that growth would not come about without opposition. The parable of the weeds (Matthew 13) reveals the existence of an enemy who will try to pollute and confuse the harvest.

In sending out his disciples, Jesus clearly demonstrated his concern to bring in the lost sheep of the house of Israel (Matthew 10). The great commission like wise, reveals that the desire of the King is that the Kingdom

---

[106] David Burnett, *The Healing of the Nations*, Paternoster, Carlisle, 1986, p. 142.

should increase (Matthew 16:18).[107] Growth is therefore an integral part of the Kingdom and also of the church. The church here on earth has a special role to invite people to accept Christ as their master and saviour and should acknowledge that God the Father, Son and Holy Spirit has entrusted all the task of mission and evangelism to her.

Thus in light of the above scriptural evidence we can easily see that the Church of God should grow for the sake of God's Kingdom. But our concern should be in 'what ways does growth occur' and 'by what means.' It is wise to note what Burnett has contributed to the study of missions that any growth has two sets of factors: 'the particular people attached to the church' and 'the commitment to the aims of the church.'[108] Thus in this scenario we have what we call 'quantitative growth' and 'qualitative growth'. When we look at how the Christian faith has been passed on through the ages, it is advisable to critically analyze whether the church experienced 'quantitative growth' or 'qualitative growth' or both as it was spreading. Christian Church membership can increase by doing missionary work, evangelism, church ministries of spiritual gifts, social services to the people.

A survey of Christian missions has revealed that there is no nation which has no religion in the world. But most of the religions of humankind have been local or even tribal in their character.[109] Of the three missionary religions; Christianity, Islam and Buddhism, Christianity has succeeded in becoming the most universal religion. Christianity is now found in almost every race of the world.[110] It has also drawn believers from almost all religions of the world. This has come all about because of missionary work since its beginning in the first century. With this in mind, Christianity has to be preached to all generations and all people including those with their in-born religions.

---

[107] David Burnett, *The Healing of the Nations*, Paternoster, Carlisle, 1986, p. 161.
[108] David Burnett, *The Healing of the Nations*, Paternoster, Carlisle, 1986, p. 160.
[109] John Schwarz, *The Compact Guide to the Christian Faith*, Bethany House Publishers, Minneapolis, 1998, 122.
[110] This is true with most religions. Mistakably even Christianity started as a Jewish sect. After realising its uniqueness almost the whole world now knows that it is the only saving religion.

1. Missionary work during the early church expansion (30-400 AD)

The expansion of the Christian Church starts with the Apostolic era. The Apostolic era opened with the first Pentecost, following Jesus' death and resurrection when the Holy Spirit came upon Peter and other disciples in Jerusalem (Acts 2) and the conversion of other apostles like Paul (Acts 9).[111] Touched people full of the Holy Spirit went out to witness and preach the gospel starting in Jerusalem, Judea, Samaria and the end of the earth as prophesied by Jesus himself in Acts 1:8. It is important to know that the church of the first Christian generation was genuinely missionary. There were full-time missionaries such as James, Peter and then Paul and Barnabas who were set apart with prayer (Acts 13).[112] Also helpers as trained by Paul participated in missionary work (Colossians 1:17). In addition there were numerous anonymous witnesses who scattered all over Jerusalem and the Greco-Roman world. By the end of the second century there were three outstanding centres of Christianity outside Jerusalem: Antioch (a second place of Christian expansion where the disciples were first called Christians), Rome and Alexandria (first school of Theology).

The Apostolic era covers the period from Acts 2, through Christians in dispersion, the time of New Testament Canon formation, the conversion of Emperor Constantine of Rome and the Councils of Nicaea and Constantinople in 381 which formulated the basic beliefs of Christianity.[113] During this period persecution, and the controversies over doctrines of the church were regarded as the main hindrances to the Church growth.

Expansion during the Roman Empire would be of special interest to comment on. The Roman Empire created many aspects favourable to the preaching of the gospel. The Roman Empire had imposed unity and maintained peace as well as constructed roads. These aspects made travel safer and more rapid. The other useful aspect was a common language, (Koine Greek),[114] which the church adopted. It was a key language, one who knew could go anywhere and find friends to whom he would talk.

---

[111] John Schwarz, *The Compact Guide to the Christian Faith*, Bethany House Publishers, Minneapolis, 1998, p. 122.
[112] D.S. Mwakanandi, *Missiology:* TEEM Notes, p. 19.
[113] John Schwarz, *The Compact Guide to the Christian Faith*, Bethany House Publishers, Minneapolis, 1998, p. 124.
[114] Mwakanandi, *Missiology*: TEEM Notes, p. 19.

Probably a more important factor was the presence of Jews in large numbers in every part of the Empire. Most of them were trained in Old Testament. Their monotheistic Jewish religion provided good ground for Christianity. It was with the group of the Jewish proselytes and God-fearers that preaching of the gospel found its most ready and most immediate response (Acts 13:16). It was easier for them to accept Christianity because Gentiles could be admitted without undergoing the rite of circumcision. Survey of the course of events in lying Roman Empire the general impression is of one rapid progress.

However, the modern missiologists are aware that the declaration of Christianity as an official religion in Rome by Emperor Constantine resulted in spiritual decline of the Christian church. While numerically church membership increased, immorality, lack of commitment to their call and syncretism among Christians were rampant. It is sad to point out that even the clerical members' spirituality drastically declined. Spirituality was so low that the Emperor had a bigger influence compared to the clerics.[115]

Nevertheless, Christianity latter was spread to many places within the Empire, like Gaul and Spain, Egypt, Cyrene, North Africa and then outside the Roman Empire to countries like America, Georgia, India and Ethiopia.

It was only when the Barbarians and Muslims attached the following centuries that Christianity in the Roman Empire declined.

2. *Missionary work in the Middle Ages (5th -15th centuries)*

The Roman Empire in the west lasted for more than 1,200 years from 753 BC to AD 476.[116] The Middle Ages span from the end of the Roman Empire up to the last half of the 15th Century. There were a number of negative factors which hindered the missionary work during this period. There were four big stumbling blocks. *Firstly*, several attacks on Roman Empire took place from as early as the 3rd Century. But, from 410 up to 476 serious attacks took place which marked the fall of the west Roman Empire under the leadership of Romulus Augustus. The ravage was done by Germanic people who lived beyond the Danube and Rhine called 'the Barbarians' like Vandals, Visigoths, the Anglo Saxons invaded the Empire. The Barbarians

---

[115] W.H.C. Frend, *The Early Church*, pp. 146-150 reports how influential Emperor Constantine was on the formulation of church doctrine.

[116] Jon Schwarz, *The Compact Guide to Christian Faith*, Bethany Minneapolis, 1998, p. 124.

became the new political leaders.[117] Later on the Muslims also came and ravaged some parts of the Empire like Jerusalem, Carthage, Spain and others. This is also called the '*Dark Ages.*' Christianity was seriously affected in many ways. It made the situation even worse as we know that prior and during this period there the doctrinal controversies and the formulation of church doctrines (325-481). *Secondly*, there was the Schism between East and West in 1054. At that time the Western Church stood in need of a radical reformation which came from the ranks of monasticism.[118] *Thirdly,* there was the decline in the Papacy, in 1303. *Fourthly*, the fall of Constantinople in 1453 when it was attacked by the Ottoman Turks because of weak leadership, moral decay, and Roman inability to finance.[119] We can note that wars from within and outside, spiritual slackness, divisions among Christians, controversies, power competition can also be disastrous to missions.

What about Augustine? No missionary historian can start commenting about Middle Age Christianity without the mention of *Augustine of Hippo*. Thus before we give some short details of Middle Ages events, we should briefly say something about Augustine (354-430). Probably as John Schwarz has notably argued that "Augustine represents a transitional or hinge figure between the early church and the beginning of the middle age church, much as Martin Luther stands between the end of the middle age church and the modern church,"[120] it does not give a surprise if a brief comment on his theological contribution to the mission and growth of the church can be presented.

Augustine fought against the heretical *Manicheans* who believed that there were two deities in God, one good and one evil, who were at war with one another. Augustine came to believe and taught that there was one God, who was good and powerful and that evil came not from God but from the misuse of the free will. All true believers strongly believe, maintain and preach that evil never comes from God who is holy and loving.

Augustine also fought against the *Donatists* who believed the validity of the sacraments depended on the moral character of the priest who administered them. Augustine defended the Church, no matter what its imperfec-

---

[117] D.S. Mwakanandi, *Missiology*: TEEM Notes, p. 22.
[118] John Schwarz, *The Compact Guide to the Christian Faith*, p. 126.
[119] Justo L. Gonzalez, *Church History: Essential Guide*, Nashville, Abingdon, 1996, p. 41-67.
[120] John Schwarz, *Christian Faith*, p. 125.

tions, as the vehicle of God's grace. Yes, sacraments as "holy signs and seals of the covenant of grace directly instituted by God to present Christ and his benefits and to conform our participation in him, their validity,"[121] cannot depend on the celebrant. However, the moral quality and uprightness of the celebrant is very significant not only to the participants but more importantly to God who calls everybody especially those who directly act on his behalf- the church leaders. The immorality of leadership can impact greatly on followers, as Jesus teaches about the blind person leading another blind person (Matthew 15:14).

Augustine also fought against the *Pelagians*, who believed that men and women were not born sinful and they could, through the exercise of their wills, live a sinless life (salvation by merit). Augustine said that because of the fall, sin is part of the human condition. "Augustine stressed that man is born not as a blank sheet of paper, but sin. Man has no free will which enables him to choose the good examples, but chained will that has to be liberated by God. Man is not saved by his own choice, but by God in Christ. Grace is not dispensable for those who make good choices, but indispensable because only God's gracious gift in Christ redeems and liberates."[122] Indeed, Pelagianism had to be condemned by a church council at Ephesus in 431.[123]

In the 600s a new force emerged on the world scene when the prophet Muhammad launched a new religion, *Islam*. Following Muhammad's death in 632, North Africa and into Spain in early 700s, challenging Christianity.[124] Since then Islam is the world's second largest religion and Christianity greatest competitor. We will discuss Missionary work to Muslims later. The main categories on Middle aged are marked by the following characteristics.

The Catholic- Orthodox Schism (1054)

This was yet another big challenge for the Christian church created by Christians themselves. The church historians will very well remember that two great divisions occurred in Christianity. The first took place in 1054 when the Eastern or Byzantine church in Constantinople separated from the

---

[121] Rowland S. Ward (ed), *The Westminster Confession and Catechisms in Modern English*, Victoria, New Melbourne Press, 2001, p. 55.
[122] Stephen Paas, *A Conflict on Authority in the Early African Church. Augustine of Hippo and the Donatists*, Zomba, 2000, p. 14.
[123] John Schwarz, *Church History*, p. 125.
[124] D.S. Mwakanandi, *Missiology:* TEEM Notes, p. 22.

Western Church in Rome (Great Schism). The second took place in 1517 when the Western Church further divided into Catholic and Protestant (Reformation).[125]

We can also recall that before 1054, the Western and Eastern churches were already separated by distance between Rome and Constantinople, which was very long-about 1000 miles apart. They also spoke different languages- the West spoke Latin and the East spoke Greek and they had different authorities- the West followed the Pope while the East followed the decisions of the first ecumenical councils. However it is of great significance if we note some important differences in a more detailed way. Schwarz lists three differences.[126]

1. The Eastern Church did not accept the *Pope* as the head of the Church. It regarded all bishops as equals of which the bishop was of Constantinople the first among the equals, but not supreme.

2. The controversy on the Spirit and the Godhead. The Eastern church believed that the *Holy Spirit* proceeded from the Father through the Son, where as the Western Church believed that the Spirit proceeded from the Father (John 14:26) and the Son (Luke 24:49), a tenet that was added to the Nicene Creed by the Western Church at the non-ecumenical Council in 589.

3. The Eastern Church venerated i*cons* (holy images)-paintings of Jesus, Mary and the Saints that were used for devotions and as teaching devices.

In the year 1054, Pope Leo IX excommunicated Cerularius for overstepping his authority. Cerularius had the favour of the Christian church and the Church was split into two halves. The Roman Catholic Church, owed its allegiance to the Pole in Rome and claiming to be the Catholic or Universal Church and the other half the Orthodox Church insisting on the true and correct faith.[127]

It is known by many church history readers that the Orthodox Church is known as Eastern or Greek Orthodox. The Orthodox have patriarchs in important cities like Jerusalem, Alexandria and Moscow, called Metropolitans. They have archbishops, and bishops, but no Pope or Papacy. The Clergy may marry or not. They maintain the seven sacraments called 'Holy mysteries' of which Baptism and Eucharist are the most important.

---

[125] John Schwarz, *Christian Faith*, p. 127.
[126] John Schwarz, *The Compact Guide to the Christian Faith*, p. 127.
[127] John Schwarz, *The Compact Guide to the Christian Faith*, p. 127.

Another important period in Christian expansion is the time of the *Crusades (1095-1291)*. The name crusade comes from the Latin word *'crux,'* meaning *'cross,'* which the crusaders wore on their clothing and shields. The Crusades were 200 years (1095-1291) of campaigns launched to expel the Muslims from the Holy Land.[128] Thus Christianity spread here by war. Of all Crusades the first was the most successful, recapturing Jerusalem in 1099. The other Crusades were not successful and many ended in disgrace and dishonour as the crusaders turned their attention from recapturing the holy places of Christendom to pillaging or plundering, rape and murder.

During the same period (1225-1274), there arose *Thomas Aquinas* who was believed to be the greatest thinker and theologian of his time. His teaching affected the church. He attempted to construct a synthesis between biblical and revealed theology and natural theology (reason) believing that it was possible through reason to come to the knowledge of God. His theology has still great influence in the present Roman Catholic Church.

In the Twelfth Century, *Monasticism* was born and expanded as a response to the church's institutionalization.[129] It taught and encouraged one's devotion to Jesus by living a life of prayer, study, meditation and fasting Celibacy as a sign of holiness became the norm for clerics.

Religious Orders became most important Catholic during the Middle Ages. The Order of St Francis were founded in 1209, Dominican Order of Preachers was founded in 1215 by Dominic of Castle of Spain. Then came the Society of Jesus, which became the largest and the strongest order in the Roman Catholic Church.[130]

3. Missionary Work after the Protestant Reformation (1500s-1800)

The Reformation - the effort to reform the Church - split the Western Church in half: Catholic and Protestant. The principal protests were:

1. The Papal system, which concentrated power in the pope and the curia, the bureaus and agencies used by the Pope to administer the church.

2. The immorality and corruption and of the clergy, many of whom used their positions as avenues for personal gain.

---

[128] John Schwarz, *The Compact Guide to the Christian Faith*, p. 128.
[129] John Schwarz, *The Compact Guide to the Christian Faith*, p. 129.
[130] John Schwarz, *The Compact Guide to the Christian Faith*, p. 129.

3. The church's oppression, the most violent form being the Spanish Inquisition, instituted in 1478 to examine a person's suspected of heresy which imprisoned, tortured and executed thousands upon thousands.

4. The church's sale of indulgencies (written pardons) to shorten one's temporal punishment in purgatory as to enter heaven more quietly to finance various Vatican projects, such as St Peter's church in Rome.[131]

The Protestant Reformation was championed by Martin Luther (1483-1546)[132] who can correctly be called the founder of Protestantism. John Calvin (1509-1564) also influenced many Reformed Churches up to the present day.

Reformation thought and theology includes the following.

1. The Reformation relies solely on God's Word (sola scriptura) while the Roman Catholic Church gave great or equal weight to the church's teaching and tradition.

2. Salvation was by grace (sola gratia) through faith (sola fide). The Catholic Church held itself to be the exclusive channel through which God's Salvation was made available to his people through the sacraments.

3. The Priesthood of all believers which eliminated divisions between clergy and laity.

The Roman Catholic Missions in the 16th and 17th Centuries

The 16th and 17th centuries were for the Roman Catholic World a time of great and notable enterprise. What however most deeply distinguishes the two centuries is a radical change in the organization of the missions. In the 16th century the missionary initiative had been taken by the kings of Portugal and Spain. The great religious orders like the Jesuits, Franciscans and Dominicans emerged. During this time the missionary advantages included

1. Missionaries enjoyed royal protection and had no difficulty in securing passages and Portuguese ships.

2. Financial help came from the government and was in most cases generous.

3. The godly rivalry or competition between the orders tended to promote vigorous action.[133]

---

[131] John Schwarz, *The Compact Guide to the Christian Faith*, p. 130.
[132] John Schwarz, *The Compact Guide to the Christian Faith*, p. 130.
[133] Mwakanandi, *Missiology:* TEEM Notes, p. 27.

But on the other hand such organization and rivalries were grave drawbacks to the missionary work which include

I. the political connection meant that missionaries were liable to be too much engaged in secular concern and even trade.

II. the rivalry between orders was often less godly, for example in Japan, where the Franciscans bitterly criticize the Jesuits.

III. the association of the missions with Spain and Portugal meant that, in reality only a small part of the Christian world was being drawn on for support. As the missionaries grew the burden became too heavy to be borne. At the same time the powers of government were growing less.[134]

It was during Gregory XV in 1622, when a step was taken to bring in new strategy for the mission with the founding of the Sacred Congregation for the Propagation of Faith (Propaganda) was introduced. Francesco Ingoli who as the Secretary up to 1649 influenced the re-organization of the mission as follows:

1. Missionary work must be freed from the stranglehold that Spain and Portugal had been able to maintain.

2. Many more bishoprics must be created and bishops must stand in a closer relationship to Rome.

3. The particular clergy must be employed in order to keep the balance with the religious orders.

4. An indigenous clergy must be developed as rapidly as possible every part of the world.[135]

A brief survey of the Roman Catholic missionary work in the 17th and 18th century is as follows:

India

Robert de Nobili (1577-1656), a young Italian Jesuit went there in 1605. He worked in South India for 50 years. To win Indians he had to adopt a method to become an Indian by custom and practice. He was tremendously successful.

---

[134] D.S. Mwakanandi, *Missiology:* TEEM Notes, p. 27.
[135] D.S. Mwakanandi, *Missiology*: TEEM Notes, p. 28.

China

At the death of Ricci in 1656 the Jesuit mission found a successor- the German Johan Adam Schall von Bell (1591-1666). Schall von Bell went to China in 1622. He made rapid progress, by 1650 there was already a large number of baptisms. At the same time it was not always well with the mission, it had some setbacks. In 1664 the old charge that the missionaries were emissaries was brought up again and he was condemned to death with five of his assistants. The assistants were executed immediately but Schall was reprieved and died a natural death the following year.

Vietnam[136]

Alexander de Rhodes was sent to South Vietnam in 1623. He immediately mastered the Vietnamese language and had remarkable success. Because of some problems he went to North Vietnam in 1627 where he also achieved a great success.

Africa.[137]

This followed the discovery of the mouth of the Congo by Diego Cam in 1484. The Capuchins were the first to work on the West coast of Africa. Success was good, so that between 1645 and 1700 the Capuchins had baptized many people in the Congo, Angola and other areas. A few of bishoprics were established.

The Jesuits worked on the other side of Africa. They opened work in Mozambique and along the Zambezi up to Monomotapa. The Dominicans and Augustinians followed.[138]

Canada.[139]

In 1534 traveller Jacques Cartier from France, claimed possession of the country and called it New France. But real occupation by France was on 24th June 1615.

French missionaries came at once to evangelize the people. Many orders took part, but once again the Jesuits were the major order. The orders

---

[136] D.S. Mwakanandi, *Missiology:* TEEM Notes, p. 28.
[137] D.S. Mwakanandi, *Missiology*: TEEM Notes, p. 28.
[138] D.S. Mwakanandi, *Missiology:* TEEM Notes, p. 28.
[139] D.S. Mwakanandi, *Missiology*: TEEM Notes, p. 29.

expanded their work throughout the area, which is now called Canada and the United States.

South America.[140]

The most notable enterprise to evangelize South America was carried out by the Jesuits. In early years their work suffered gravely from hostility of colonialists who did not wish to see so large a proportion of the population withdrawn from their control to settle on mission settlements.[141]

The Collapse of the Roman Catholic Mission

The second half of the 18th century was a period of tragic collapse for the Roman Catholic Mission. The causes of the collapse include the following.

1. Spain and Portugal were no longer the leading powers in the world; the Pope's Bulls dividing the world between them was no longer effective. From 1600 onwards, the Protestant powers, England, Holland and Denmark began to enter what the Roman Catholic nations had regarded as their exclusive lands. By the middle of the 18th century England became the dominant power in India, and Portugal had almost ceased to count.

2. Local rulers persecuted the Christians, for example, Japanese Christianity was almost completely destroyed by persecution. Such experiences happened in other parts of the world too.

3. A final blow was the dissolution of the Jesuit order. Causes include: complaints of their arrogance, their improper missionary methods, their interference in political affairs, and vast wealth accumulated through their commercial enterprise. On 21 July 1773, Pope Clement XVI dissolved the society, removed all its property and declared that no Pope in future should ever recall it into being. At that time the society numbered 22,589 members of whom 11,293 were priests. At least 3,000 missionaries were immediately withdrawn from their fields, put on board ship like cattle and carried of to their country off origin.[142]

Protestant missions in the 16th and 17th centuries

In contrast to the Roman Catholics, there was little sign of any urge among the reformers to do missionary work in the 16th and 17th centuries. It is a

---

[140] D.S. Mwakanandi, *Missiology*: TEEM Notes, p. 29.
[141] D.S. Mwakanandi, *Missiology*: TEEM Notes, p. 29.
[142] D.S. Mwakanandi, Missiology: TEEM Notes, p. 30.

strange fact that the Reformers neglected missionary work in practice and doctrine. The following reasons are often given to account for the lack of missionary activity in the Protestant churches of the Reformation.[143]

1. Their lack of contact with heathens and with Islam. The Protestant people of Europe entered the colonial era much later than Portugal and Spain (the Roman Catholic super powers). It was only after the founding of the Dutch East India Company in 1602 that attempts were made to do missionary work through the ministers and sick comforters who worked on the ships and in colonial areas.

2. Because of the great power of Roman Catholicism and the division in the protestant ranks, Protestantism in Europe was for long time concerned only with its own desperate struggle for existence.

3. Certain theological and especially eschatological misconceptions among the Reformers, for example, their idea that the command to do mission work had been meant *ad personam* for the Apostles only (Matthew 28:18-20) and their belief that Christ's second coming was at hand (Mark 1:1-14)

4. Protestant monarchs were completely lacking in interest in mission work.

5. The religious wars caused set-backs which rendered the Protestant people powerless.

6. The Protestant Churches lacked the orders which were used in Roman Catholicism for missionary work.[144]

The first Protestant Theologian to plead for missionary work was Hadrian Saravia (1531-1613). The following were the main factors in determining the development of the Protestant mission.

I. The colonial and commercial development of the Protestant peoples. In India Protestantism only arrived in the 17th century in the person of Dutch, British and Danish.

II. Protestant monarchs now realized that they bore the responsibility to mission work. Thus during the 16th century Gustav Vasa of Sweden was one of the first monarchs to send out missionaries, and during the 18th century, Fredric IV of Denmark launched the mission in Tranquebar in India.

---

[143] D.S. Mwakanandi, *Missiology:* TEEM Notes, p. 30.
[144] D.S. Mwakanandi, *Missiology:* TEEM Notes, p. 30.

III. New life broke through the rigid dogmatism of the 17th century in the Pietism and Puritanism of Europe, Britain and America.[145]

In summary, during the 16th century there were a few attempts at Protestant missionary activity, but Protestant work, only flourished after the coming of the Great awakening in 1834

4. The modern missionary movement (18th -21st centuries)

Before coming to the missionary movements after the 18th century it would be important to mention that during the 18th century, the missions in both the Roman Catholic and Protestants churches reached a low water mark. To this states of affairs in the case of the Roman Catholic church contributed, among others; rationalism of the 18th century, the French Revolution, the suffering of the Pope at the hands of Napoleon and the abolition of the Jesuits.[146]

In the Protestant churches of the 18th century, the vision and the conviction that they had a missionary obligation was still very faint. Only a few missionary efforts were started mainly in the revivalist circles of Pietism and Puritanism.

But during the 19th century the position changed radically both in Roman Catholic and Protestant churches. It became the great century of missionary and expansion. To the development of *the modern missionary movement* many factors contributed.

1. Mechanical inventions e.g. transport, travel and communication.

2. The colonial expansion especially of the British, but also the Dutch, French, Belgian and German people opened the way for thousands of missionaries.

3. The developing trade and commerce between countries contributed to missions.

4. During the 19th century also developed in the churches an unprecedented sense of obligation to carry the gospel to all the nations. Hence evangelical revivals took place.

5. One of the results of the revival movement was the establishment of missionary societies.[147]

---

[145] D.S. Mwakanandi, *Missiology*: TEEM Notes, p. 31.
[146] D.S. Mwakanandi, *Missiology*: TEEM Notes, p. 32.
[147] D.S. Mwakanandi, *Missiology*: TEEM Notes, p. 33.

Missionary methods of the 19th century

To meet the demands of different situations, a variety of missionary methods was used both in Roman Catholic and Protestant Churches.

1. Preaching and teaching were the most important method. Church and school marched together.
2. Very early medical missions were used as a method of spreading the Gospel.
3. Agricultural and industrial institutions were established to promote development
4. Printing presses to disseminate information through publications were established.

The missionary pioneers studied the language of the indigenous people. Many languages were reduced to writing.

Roman Catholic Missions

It is worth noting that initially, the Roman Catholic Church dismissed the Reformers as minor irritants. When the Reformation began to spread and take root, the Catholic Church was compelled to meet it head on and called the Council of Trent. This Council has been regarded by Roman Catholics as the most important council between the council of Nicaea (325) and Vatican II (1962-65). At its meetings it reaffirmed Roman Catholic Doctrines challenged by the Protestants; reaffirmed the Church as the official interpreter of scripture; confirmed Septuagint books in the Catholic Canon; increased papal authority over the Church; and condemned and abolished certain abuses, including the sale of indulgences. The Church also thought of intensifying missionary work through its Orders as Protestants became their competitors.

Thus Roman Catholic also sent numerous missionaries internationally and worldwide. Wherever they went they did not only preach. They also established schools, theological institutions and intensified their charitable works. France in particular contributed a lot to Roman Catholic Missions. Spain followed then Belgium, Holland, Ireland and later America and Britain. Missionary expedition abroad were restarted. Some missionaries were sent to China in 1860, Japan in 1859; Africa in 1848, 1856, 1868; south Africa in

1863; West Africa and Sierra Leone, Dahomey and Nigeria. They were especially successful in Cameroon and also in the Congo.[148]

The Protestant missions

The Awakening of the missionary spirit came from the Great Awakening. The first important missionary of the Methodists was Thomas Cook. He was sent to visit Methodists in America. His contact with Negro slaves inspired the idea of mission to Africa and in 1804 the mission in North Africa with Gibraltar as headquarters was started under his leadership. In 1811, missionary work began in Sierra Leone, in 1813, he led a mission to Ceylon and Indonesia but he died on the voyage.[149]

William Carey

The modern Protestant missionary movement began with William Carey. From what we have discussed above, he was not the first Protestant missionary, but rather he marks the entry of the English Speaking world on a large scale into the missionary enterprise- and it has been the English-speaking world which has provided four-fifths of the non-Roman Catholic missionaries from the days of Carey to the present day.[150] Stephen Neil (A History of Christian Missions), also highlights the same point.

Schwarz summarizes Carey's missionary story as follows

> Carey was born in 1761 in Northamptonshire, England. He was converted in 1779 and became a Baptist preacher in 1783. In 1792, he published a book, called the 'Enquiry' in which he introduces his ideas about missionary work to the heathens. He helped form the Baptist Missionary Society and then set out for India, arriving in Calcutta in 1793. Carey immersed himself in Indian life and thought; lived in a Danish compound in Serampore (beyond the control of the British East India Company in Calcutta, which opposed Christian missions); earned money in a dyestuff factory; and learned several Indian languages. His motto was "Attempt great things for God and expect great things from God".
>
> Carry supervised complete and twenty-four partial translations of the Bible into Indian languages; wrote Indian language dictionaries and grammars; co-founded Serampore College, the first Christian College in Asia; founded the Agricultural Society of India to promote agricultural improvements; started

---

[148] D.S. Mwakanandi, *Missiology: TEEM Notes*, p. 34.
[149] D.S. Mwakanandi, *Missiology:* TEEM Notes, p. 34.
[150] Schwarz, *The Compact Guide to the Christian Faith*, p. 135.

what is now the largest news paper in India, and campaigned successfully against Hindu practice of widows cremating themselves on their husband's funeral pyres.[151]

Church historian Ruth Tucker said, in writing about Carey, 'More than any other individual in modern history, Carey stirred the imagination of the Christian world and showed by his own humble example what could and should be done to bring a lost world to Christ.' Carey never returned to England, dying in India in 1834 at seventy three."[152] We cannot talk about modern protestant missions without the mention of Carey.

---

[151] Schwarz, *The Compact Guide to the Christian Faith*, p. 135.
[152] Schwarz, *The Compact Guide to the Christian Faith*, p. 137.

Chapter 8

Classical and faith missions

Classical Missions

William Carey has been well recognized as one of the greatest missionaries since the Apostolic days and has often been referred to as the 'Father of Modern Missions.[153] His main aim was to preach to the heathens. His missionary record has been already discussed in the preceding chapter. Carey had his own approach to the missionary work as opposed to the former one of the established Protestant Churches. To fulfill his aim he advocated the sending of missionaries as a means of propagating the gospel to the heathens abroad. He discouraged the Calvinistic theology of pre-destination which discouraged evangelization. He twisted his theology into action. His sermon on Isaiah 54 (Expect great things from God and attempt great things for God) inspired many people.[154]

All the classical missions that emerged followed Carey's approach to missionary work. Classical missions were divided into two main divisions: the denominational one to which the Baptist Missionary Society belonged which were named after the denominational origin; the interdenominational ones to which the London Missionary Society belonged which were named after the geographical origin.[155]

It is interesting to note that the structure and organization of classical missions was so different from the established protestant churches. Societies started by subscription since they were voluntary associations. The members were mostly self supporting without depending on churches or organizations, but gifts and sponsorship from well wishers.[156] The voluntary association was not restricted to ecclesiastics or to any profession, but combining all classes of people whether men or women provided they showed commitment

---

[153] H. Kane, *The Concise History of the Christian World Mission*, 1982, p. 95.
[154] Andrew Walls, "The Missionary Society and the Fortunate Subversion of the Church," *Evangelical Quarterly*, p. 1.
[155] Klaus Fiedler, *The Story of Faith Missions*, Oxford, 1994, p. 11.
[156] K.M Finnie, *William Carey by Trade a Cobbler*, England, 1986, p. 45.

to the task. Members were expected to be instrumental, people whose hearts were serious about missionary work.[157] From the voluntary members, a committee might be appointed to gather information, collect funds, scrutinize possible missionaries and equip them for their work. They were also responsible for the publishing of what they considered to be important for the world to know especially those concerning the word of God and what they were doing.[158] What was very interesting is that in their committee it is said that there was no one looking superior to the others as it might have been in the case of established churches where there was a clear hierarchical structure. They all shared ideas in a mutual and friendly manner. They were people of some cohesion, mutual trust and fellowship.

Their theological peculiarities

The theological approach of the classical missions was different from that of the Calvinistic established churches which taught that missionary work was for the Apostles.[159] The societies influenced by Carey believed that the missionary work was for every Christian. The Great commission should not be restricted to the Apostles who had received the commissioning word from Jesus.

The classical missions wanted to have their machinery, which was neglected by the established churches, to fulfill the task they wanted to carry out. Thus they subverted all the classical forms of the church government while fitting comfortably into non of them. They were not restricted to ecclesiastics, as such, they broke the theological barriers which were created by churches so much so that many people came to realize that such barriers were stumbling blocks to missionary work. Unlike the established churches, the classical missionary societies emphasized the evangelization of the whole world which was beyond the capacities of these splendid system of gospel truth. Therefore, all Christians were invited to the missionary work.[160]

In that they were not restricted to the ecclesiastics, the societies also indirectly changed the power base of churches.[161] For instance, the Baptist Missionary Society was the first society which made some of the laity of real

---

[157] K.M Finnie, *William Carey by Trade a Cobbler*, England, 1986, p. 49.
[158] K.M Finnie, *William Carey by Trade a Cobbler*, England, 1986, p. 59.
[159] Louise Pirouet, *Christianity World Wide: Church History*, Great Britain, 1978, p. 129.
[160] Louise Pirouet, *Christianity World Wide: Church History*, Great Britain, 1978, p. 131.
[161] Justo, Gonzalez, *The Story of Christianity*, Abingdon Press, Nashville, 1983, 306.

significance above parish or congregation. The societies used those people whether priests or laymen who had been neglected by their churches. The Church Missionary Society which came to West Africa was initially started by a group of 'ecclesiastical nobodies'. They never asked for permission from the church officials like bishops to start societies.[162] They were strongly convinced that the Great Commission from Jesus Christ was not meant to be conditioned by yes or no from the church officials lest they might be hindrances to the mission. The Societies are also credited for working tooth and nail to reform the manners of the nations by rebuking profanity and seeking to keep prostitutes off the streets. They tirelessly preached against social injustices especially the slave trade.[163] The spirit extended even to Africa. Missionaries to Africa taught against the evils of the slave trade.

While established churches believed very much in the ordination of the clergy, to some of the classical missions ordination was secondary.[164] Any Christian was encouraged to participate in missionary work while in the established churches priority was given to the ordained ministers of word and sacrament. Classical missions were also less concerned about doctrines. They could be more widely interdenominational. Women who had been neglected by established churches were so instrumental to reach the unreached. For Example Mary Moffat the wife of Robert Moffat did a lot of mission work and contributed a lot to Christianization of the southern part of Africa, particularly at Kuruman.

Some Activities in Africa

Of the Malawian classical missions, much missionary activities must be credited to, the London Missionary Society which operated much in Southern Africa and to the Church Missionary Society which was very active in West Africa. However some like the Methodists, the Basle Mission and others also contributed to missionary work in Africa. In West Africa, Christianity owes its origin to Sierra Leone where missionaries sent by the Church Missionary Society came in 1804. The first missionaries who came earlier than 1804 had been held at bay because of mosquitoes. This also contributed

---

[162] Justo Gonzalez, *The Story of Christianity*, Abingdon Press, Nashville, 1983, p. 308.
[163] S. Lamin, *West African Christianity*, Great Britain, p. 60.
[164] S. Lamin, *West African Christianity*, Great Britain, p. 61.

to their failure even more in the area of pastoral work. Gradually after the arrival of the CMS in 1804, the missionaries entered the interior of Africa and Sierra Leona became a Christian country in 1827 with a mission station at Fourah Bay.[165] Several churches and schools were established. The success of the missionary work in this particular area has been associated to the abundance of freed slaves, some of whom came from North America.[166] In 1828, the Basle Mission Association entered Ghana with the Danish Trading Company. They arrived at the coast and latter penetrated into the interior. In the first instance they faced problems in settling because the found a very poor and divided people. Later a notable work was done. Apart from the word of God, education, scientific studies and agriculture were introduced.[167] Freed slaves became very instrumental in the Christianization of Ghana. Latter freed slaves as already converted Christians from Sierra Leone made their way and entered Nigeria upon invitation made by their fellow freed slaves in Nigeria. By 1842, Methodists and Anglicans (among them Samuel Ajaji an African missionary), under the leadership of Henry Townsend evangelized Nigeria. Samuel Ajaji became a missionary to Nigeria in 1844. The most famous Scottish lady worth mentioning is Mary Slessor who apart from preaching was very strong at condemning civil wars. She was also referred to as the Queen of Calabar.[168]

East Africa. In Uganda it was the chief Kabaka Mtesa who called for CMS to protect his Kingdom from Egypt.[169] The missionaries came in 1877, converted the King and some of the natives then established churches. However Christianity declined when the king died and the son who succeeded was not a committed Christian. The Muslims and some of the natives revolted against Christianity accusing them of being a political movement. A great persecution took place and Christianity drastically declined.[170] In Tanzania and Kenya including Zanzibar, the CMS was introduced by David Livingstone who when he heard about slave trading operating especially among the Nyamwezi and Ngoni sought of introducing another trade to replace the slave trade. He attracted missionaries to come to Zanzibar which,

---

[165] S. Lamin, *West African Christianity*, Great Britain, p. 62.
[166] Stephen Neill, *A History of Christian Mission*, Penguin, Harmondsworth, 1964, p. 260.
[167] Stephen Neill, *A History of Christian Mission*, Penguin, Harmondsworth, 1964, p. 261.
[168] Stephen Neill, *A History of Christian Mission*, Penguin, Harmondsworth, 1964, p. 262.
[169] Stephen Neill, *A History of Christian Mission*, Penguin, Harmondsworth, 1964, p. 263.
[170] Stephen Neill, *A History of Christian Mission*, Penguin, Harmondsworth, 1964, p. 263.

latter declared the slave trade illegal. In 1874, the CMS opened a settlement at Mombasa with some evangelists like David George. and William Jones who were later ordained as African priests. Unfortunately in East Africa, freed slaves were disturbed by Muslims to be converted to Christianity. But later some were converted and took part in preaching and teaching in churches.[171]

Southern Africa. The London Missionary Society first settled at the Cape where it found the Moravians already there. The LMS first came under the leadership of James Read. who was later succeeded by John Philip. They had their settlement at Betheldorp. Following evangelization, they taught people how to support themselves by introducing agriculture and trade. Although the LMS had taught Toyo Soga as a pastor who established a church at Mungwali and a school at Lovedale, it was not very successful because of the bad relationship between the white missionaries and the coloureds.[172]

The effective famous missionaries were Robert and Mary Moffat (1797-1883) They settled at Kuruman and served in Africa for 48-50 years. The Moffats had a good relationship with the chiefs like Moshweshwe. This enabled them to be successful missionaries. They translated the Bible into the Tswana language and the birth was printed for the first time in Africa at Kuruman Press. They introduced schools. They also taught improved methods of farming and commerce. The Moffats were followed by David Livingstone who responded to Moffat's appeal that Africa needed more missionaries. During his exploration of Southern Africa, then going northwards he reached many people including chiefs. As a medicine man he introduced medicine. He also substituted slave trade with trade in goods. Through his exploration, Livingstone opened the way for more missions to come to Central and East Africa: In 1861, the Universities Mission to Central Africa (UMCA). 1875 the Fee Church of Scotland, in 1876 the Church of Scotland, in 1886, the Dutch Reformed Church and many more.[173]

In summary and in light of the classical mission societies, I would like to conclude by saying, to be a Christian is to be a missionary. And to be a missionary it to fulfill the work of discipleship. This discipleship is not con-

---

[171] Stephen Neill, *A History of Christian Mission*, Penguin, Harmondsworth, p. 266.

[172] J. Weller and J Linden, *Mainstream Christianity in Malawi, Zambia and Zimbabwe, Zimbabwe*, Gweru: Mambo Press, 1984, pp. 11-12.

[173] J. Weller and J Linden, *Mainstream Christianity,* Gweru: Mambo Press, 1884, pp. 10-48.

cerned with theory but much more with practice. Effective discipleship is that which is not just professional but voluntary.

Faith Missions

While classical missions occurred from 1792 onwards, Faith missions started In 1865. Classical and Faith Missions have much in common First Faith Mission was the famous China Inland Mission (now Overseas Inland Missionary Fellowship) founded by Hudson Maria Taylor in 1865.[174] Many church historians and missiologists like Klaus Fiedler clearly indicate that Taylor is the most important person to leave his imprint on the faith missions.[175] The aim of Hudson Taylor was to present the gospel everywhere so that everyone has a chance to hear or read it and to accept Christ as Saviour. Parallel to this was the conviction that Christ's second coming will only take place after the gospel has been preached to all people.

Some scholars like Kane would support the idea that the term Faith Missions has been applied to a number of interdenominational agencies which were born as a result of responses and answers received from prayers they relied on. In other words, Faith Missions looked to the Lord for the supply of their needs. But "they themselves however would be the last to claim that they had monopoly of faith."[176] Their missionaries had no guaranteed income though they do have support scale which they try to maintain. They did not go into debts nor did they solicit funds. They prefer to make their needs known to Christian public and look.[177] While sometimes the mainstream denominations had rivalries, faith missions just did their work as sent by God. They never regarded themselves as being in competition with the main line denomination. But mistakably, the main line denominational missions have tended to regard the faith missions as something of what Kane calls "'Cinderella' and referred to them as 'sects'"[178] To reaffirm their seriousness and commitment, faith mission had a statement of faith which each member was expected to sign. In this way they also preserved their

---

[174] Herbert Kane, *A Concise History of Christian World Mission*, Grand Rapids, Baker Book House, p. 95.
[175] Klaus Fiedler, *Story of Faith Missions*, Regnum Books, Oxford, 1994, pp. 11-25.
[176] Hebert Kane, *A Concise History of Christian World Mission*, Grand Rapids, Baker Book House, 1987, p. 101.
[177] Herbert Kane, *A Concise History of the World Mission*, Grand Rapids-Baker Book House.
[178] Herbert Kane, *A Concise History of the Christian World Mission*, p. 102.

conservative and evangelical stance.[179] Such being the case the Faith Missions grew tremendously and attracted many people.

Throughout the years the Faith Missions have derived most of their support from the independent Bible, Baptist and community churches and their recruits from the Bible schools. In their overseas work they concentrated on evangelism and church planting. In the medical field, they have maintained numerous hospitals and clinics. In the education field they have put in place and maintained thousands of elementary schools, especial in Africa, but few high schools and colleges. In Theological education they have been content with Bible schools.

However, it must be briefly commented, that before the demise of colonialism, Christianity was regarded as a foreign religion which came with the western colonizers. It grew but not as fast. After independence which started as early as 1945, Christianity in most third world countries grew much faster. Churches were no longer tied to their mother churches. Leadership had also been localized. In the situation the church grew. Although Christianity was shaken by World War II and the Rise of Communism, missionary means were intensified and more were established like Short Term Programmes which targeted the youth. Kane notes that this started as a preparatory work before one becomes a career missionary. For example in the 1960 the American Society started sending young students overseas under the auspices of some mission board. Students war volunteers and paid their own transport. When students came back from summer missionary experience they share their experiences and enthusiasm with their fellow students. This has been broadened and is practiced by many denominations both evangelical and mainline. Missionaries are sent worldwide either as exchange visitors or as evangelizing means.[180] Missionary radio was introduced. This was first introduced in 1931 in the city of Quito. The Far East Broadcasting Company was established in 1945 in Manila. This extended to many parts of the world including Liberia, Korea, Swaziland, Ethiopia which was started in 1977. Bible Correspondence Courses, were introduced along with radio broadcasting. Through this facility millions of people have been enrolled in theological courses.

---

[179] Herbert Kane, *A Concise History of the Christian World Mission*, Grand Rapids, 1987, p. 102.
[180] Herbert Kane, *A Concise History of the World Christian Mission*, pp. 103-107.

The Faith mission strategy has opened the way to many interdenominational revival meetings, Bible study groups, and many charismatic movements, have invaded the mainline denomination including the Roman Catholic Church.[181] As a result of this charismatic movement influenced by the faith missions in one way or another, there are many Bible Study groups in homes, markets, shops and not forgetting secondary schools and colleges. These do happen without any human leader's effort or organization but the Holy Spirit. One will also witness the abundance of literature world wide. Bodies like Christian Literature Crusade, Evangelical Literature, Every Home Crusade are busy printing and publishing Christian literature so that the word reaches as many people as possible. Through such means many students and participants ended up in theological training to be missionaries.

Missionaries have always given high respect to *William Carey* and *William Ward* for their contribution to Christian literature. They were the greatest writers of their time regarding the spreading of the gospel to the whole world.

Faith Missions in Africa

The transfer of faith missions to Africa was effected by the Irish couple Fanny and Grattan Guinness.[182] As theologians belonging to the famous Guinness family, they spread the idea of faith missions by establishing a missionary training institution. After being refused to join Taylor in China who prior to application came to lecture his students, they went to Paris where they did their missionary work. In the long run, Hudson Tailor's advice led them to found the East London Training Institute (1873).[183]

Out of the Guinness' Institute, four faith missions were born of which Livingstone Inland Mission and Congo Balolo mission were the direct responsibility of the Institute. When these missions came to Africa they found that Christianity had already been planted by the Protestant classical missions but their distribution was uneven. The faith missions therefore settled in the unreached areas. Some of these areas were in: Central Nigeria, Morocco, Algiers, Central Africa, Congo Basin.[184] Scholars like Fiedler have

---

[181] Herbert Kane, *A Concise History of the World Christian Mission,* Grand Rapids, 1987, p. 109-112.
[182] Klaus Fiedler, *Story of Faith Missions*, Oxford, Regnum Books, 1994, p. 34.
[183] Klaus Fiedler, *Story of Faith Missions*, Oxford, Regnum Books, 1994, p. 37.
[184] Klaus Fiedler, *Story of Faith Missions*, Oxford, Regnum Books, 1994, p. 73.

reported that they were welcome in these areas because they tried to answer the needs which the classical missions had perceived but not addressed.

Guinness sent Samuel Bill to establish an independent mission in Calabar Coast in Nigeria where the first missionaries prior to classical missions had not reached so the Qua Iboe Mission was established. George Pearse and the friends of Guinness were also sent in 1881 and founded the North Africa Mission. Some smaller missions were founded, the Central Morocco and the Algiers Mission. All these were interdenominational missions. Harry Guinness started the Congo Balolo Mission in order to renew the advance into the interior continue work of Livingstone Inland Mission. Another missionary who should not be left out in Faith Mission to Africa is A.B. Simpson who was influenced by Guinness in Canada in 1843. As a fully trained Presbyterian pastor he started training missionaries in his newly founded church in the New York Missionary Institute. In 1884 he sent first missionaries to the mouth of Congo which failed because of the insufficient preparation and equipment. Fredrick Franson also failed. Latter on he succeeded when he sent his missionaries with a Scandinavian missionary, society (TEAM). Another group of missionaries went to South Africa.

In the first place Faith Missions achieved very little as compared to classical missions. However latter things began to change with the three largest Faith Missions the African Inland Mission (1895), the Sudan Inland Mission (1898) and the Sudan United Mission 1904). The other two are the Congo Inland Mission and the Heart of Africa Mission.[185] Some Faith Missions, at first they tried to have a chain of missions stations as a way of reaching the interior Africa in which they failed. Others started industrial missions where missionaries were considered to be able to support themselves through agriculture and trade. Unfortunately this also failed.[186]

Most of the African churches founded by Faith Missions' adopted believers baptism and had Presbyterian type of church government.

Theology of Faith Missions: Compare with Classical Missions.

Despite both belonging to the Protestant Missionary Movement Classical and Faith Missions have some differences although there are some similarities. Both valued the position of women in church and greatly and gave them

---

[185] Klaus Fiedler, *Story of Faith Missions*, 1994, p. 48.
[186] Klaus Fiedler, *Story of Faith Missions*, 1994, p. 320-321.

chance to participate in missionary work. Both engage themselves in Evangelism. Both stressed the values of scripture and individual conversion. And both have encouraged the system of self support. However the main contrasts are as follows:

The Concept of the Church:

Faith Missions never produced an ecclesiology of their own. They accepted the attributes of the church but gave them each a special twist. Reading Klaus Fiedler's[187] work the following points can be drawn:

I. In classical ecclesiology the corporate aspects are usually stressed but in faith missions ecclesiology the individual aspects are stressed.

II. To Faith Missions it is not the Church which creates unity but individual Christians.

III. Holiness is not a corporate aspect of the church for an individual to believe in, but a divine offer for everyone to claim individually.

IV. Catholicity of the worldwide church is not achieved by creating one church encompassing all churches in the world, but by individuals sharing and working together. The real Church is activity.

V. In Faith Missions theology passive church membership does not exist. Every church member shares in the activities of the church local and world wide. There is no speculative theology but rather applied theology. Apart from accepting holiness as a divine gift of grace the individual who wants it can take definitive steps. He or she can give up all the known sins and consciously subordinate to God's will and completely surrender himself to God.

VI. In Classical theology, the attribute of apostolicity serves more to safeguard continuity either of doctrine or power. The Faith Missions take doctrinal purity and define apostolicity as active missionary work.

VII The Faith Missions also emphasized conversion by teaching that without besides conversion, one is not a Christian. Unlike in some Classical Missions, it is not the sacrament or doctrine that makes a person a Christian but Conversion.

VIII. In the classical missions wives were not full missionaries, which in the Faith Missions they were. Single women could be independent evangelists.

---

[187] Klaus Fiedler, *Story of Faith Missions*, pp. 320-322.

In Missiology, one cannot be wrong to credit the Faith Missions. Of course, no true theologian would refute to the fact that leadership is important in the Church. Leadership brings order, guides and safeguards and defends the faith of believers. It becomes unfortunate when leadership powers have been institutionalized, abused and consequently become the stumbling blocks of the Gospel. Doctrines also help believers to understand their faith better, but it is more important to know and think about the Great Commission so that others too should hear the word of God and receive salvation. This commission is not restricted to the apostles and leadership in Church.

For the service of the Lord to be accomplished it does not need one person. It requires all believers, ordained and lay people, male and female, young and old. Like the Classical Missions, Faith Missions have contributed a lot to the church of today.

Chapter 9

New and contemporary approach to mission.

Nearly all missiologists today rightfully bear witness that almost the whole world has been reached with Christian missions. So is there need for missions? The answer to this is 'YES'. The task of mission by Christians will never stop till the Second Coming of our Lord- Jesus Christ. We must realize as Christians that so many things need the attention of the gospel. *Christian nominalism, weak Christians, syncretism, secularization, overwhelming high technology world-wide* and many more, seriously need the attention of those called Christians as they are the salt, the light and the truth of the world. But to be honest, this will really need a serious and undivided committed Christian community world wide. This requires what Jack Thompson calls 'Mission and Unity'.[188] Unfortunately, one of the biggest challenges facing Christianity as it moves towards the coming of our Lord is the challenge to have united mind and effort,[189] to fight the enemy-Satan and his evil forces who oppose the will of God and hinder the permeation of the gospel in the lives of people. Whether as one denomination or as different denominations the biggest problem that Christians are perpetually facing is that they spend time discussing their doctrinal differences and their what Millard Erickson calls 'isms'[190] which have very little or nothing to do with salvation.

Let us remind ourselves, when we study the beginning of ecumenism, those people who were sent and met as delegates at the Missionary conference in Edinburgh in 1910[191] had one common goal, to witness to Christ together as a team regardless of differences in doctrinal background, denomination and nationality. The majority of ecumenism advocates can

---

[188] Jack Thompson, "Mission into the twenty first Century", in Jack Thompson (ed), *Into all the World, History of Overseas Work of Presbyterian Church in Ireland 1840-1990*, Overseas Board, 1990.
[189] Based on the Ideas of Jack Thompson, *Into all the World*, p. 199.
[190] Based on Millard Erickson, *Christian Theology*, Grand Rapids: Baker Books, 2000, 1998 p. 1135-1155.
[191] Jack Thompson, "Mission into Twenty-First Century" in Jack Thompson (Ed), *Into All the World, The History of the Overseas Work of the Presbyterian Church in Ireland 1840-1990*, p. CI, Overseas Board, 1990.

bear witness that a lot has been achieved as far as ecumenism is concerned. Ecumenical organizations have been persuading churches to work together and numerous denominations have learned to work together and have realized the universal nature of the body of Christ and know the importance of unity in mission.

Numerous Church History books have shown how missionaries have travelled from one place to another. Like classical and faith missions of the modern post-Reformation period, missionaries have endeavoured to reach the unreached places. May missionaries have moved from Europe to Africa, Europe to America, Western Europe to Eastern Europe and Asia, from America to Africa. Also Africans have gone to preach to Europe and America. That every Christian is a missionary, there is no serious doubt about it. But if we look at what is happening and still to happen then we see that there is still need, as missiologists to continue summoning each other to work together towards the fulfillment of the great commission.[192] The science of discerning trends which will be significant in the future is a matter of urgency in as far as missiology is concerned. The Gospel should be relevant and addressing the needs of the present day. Such being the case questions like how do we go forward from here, what approach should we take, are supposed to be at the back of any missiologist's mind. Jack Thompson once an Irish missionary to Africa struggling with the issue of how to carry out missionary task today, has stated,

> so then, as we move towards the end of this millennium, we must move also into a situation where our involvement in God's mission increasingly allows Christians from all parts of the world to play their full part, as equal partners, in every aspect of that mission, and in which Christians of many different traditions come to see that the task to which they have been called is far more important than the differences that separate them [193]

In the first instance, Thompson's concern is about the changing world,[194] which also affects and influences perceptions. As the world is changing and growing socially, culturally, numerically, technologically, politically, religiously and economically those involved in the missionary task should seek ways of bringing a relevant message to the world. We really need to re-think

---

[192] Jack Thompson (ed), "Mission into the Twenty-first Century", p. 196.
[193] Jack Thompson (ed), p. 200.
[194] Jack Thompson (ed), *Mission into the Twenty-first Century*, p. 200-203.

our previous assumption so that we can fit into the present situation. Lets briefly look at some of the current challenges to the mission work.

I. *Christianity and other religions.*

The presence of many religions like Islam, Buddhism, Hinduism, African Traditional Religions, Rastafarians, Bahai, as competing religions standing on the way journeyed by Christians, is a very big challenge, particularly as some of these new religious increase much faster than Christianity.[195]

The growing figure of other religions will force missiologists increasingly to give more serious attention to critically question, evaluate and analyze the mushrooming faiths which stand side by side with Christianity. Thus while Christians are busy thinking and planning missionary approach and strategies, among other things, issues like how to convince new converts and already existing Christians that Christianity is the only true religion, how to win such indoctrinated people to Christ, are very pertinent. Christian Missionaries should be convinced themselves that Christianity is not only unique but also absolute. This is an assignment the Christians have to seriously do. There is a strong need for the missionary task to consider these other religions.

II. The issue of *ecological disaster* needs missiological attention. This has to do with both the rural and urban places. In most poor countries in Africa like Malawi, the source of energy for most of the domestic economy is coal from wood. People have no electricity, not generators to provide power. Very few people have access to technology of tapping power solar power.[196] There is also a huge increase in urbanization. Large numbers of people move from rural areas into large towns and cities. Jack Thompson reports that the famous certain missiologist, 'David Barrett estimated that while in 1900 there were only twenty cities in the world with a population of more than one million, by the year 2000 there would be 433 cities. In terms of world population this means that while in the 1900 only 230 million out of 1600 million (or one seventh) lived in towns by the year 2000, over 3000 million out of 6000 million (or one half) will be living in towns.'[197] No one would

---

[195] Jack Thompson (ed), *Mission into the Twenty-first Century*, p. 200.
[196] Forestry Department faces the biggest challenge to stop poor villagers to sell their charcoal in towns. This is not only their source of income but also the main source of energy in most African communities.
[197] Jack Thompson, *Mission into the Twenty First Century*, p. 201.

repudiate that Urbanization affects every country in the world whether developing or already developed while at the same time bearing in mind that the rate of movements differs.

While in rural areas the cutting down of trees for different purposes in homes leaves the ground bare resulting in soil erosion, reduction of fresh air, the natural beauty and others, in towns and cities air and water pollution is a serious consequence. Environmental degradation in villages/rural and towns/cities have important repercussions for mission strategies. People especially Christians must not only be involved in the spiritual welfare of the people, but also their physical welfare. Poor environment is harmful to the health of the people of God. The people of God must be responsible stewards of the environment to keep themselves healthy.[198] A saved Christian will not rejoice over the degradation of the environment which was given to him by God as a gift. He/she should be quite knowledgeable that the gift was given not only to enjoy but also to sustain it by taking care of it. Mission is not merely evangelism although evangelism is an important part of it. Jesus said 'As the Father sent me so I send you'. Thompson comments by saying "Our mission ought to be modelled on Jesus' mission. It ought to be concerned with the whole person, as well as with the environment in which God has placed us. Mission demands that in all we do we attempt (with God's help) to live by, share and work for the kingdom values."[199] It is becoming increasingly clear nowadays that any action or policy which helps to destroy God's creation is unacceptable and sinful and must strongly be opposed by Christians. Thompson adds "Christians must in fact work to make the kind of world we feel God would want, without ever giving to the temptation of thinking that we do so in our own strength."[200]

As Christians, we cannot just sit there idle without sharing our understanding of God with others. We are called by Jesus and sent to share what we have received with others. Mission is about sharing what we know about our God, not just in what we say but also in how we act, and in the values we struggle for. Most theologians agree and have advocated in their literature to take care of what we have been given as God is very much concerned injus-

---

[198] A Seminar paper on Care Takers of the Earth, Seminar Organised by Association of Christian Lay Centres in Africa, Abokobi, Accra, 2000.
[199] Jack Thompson, *Mission in the Twenty -First Century*, p. 201.
[200] Jack Thompson, *Mission in the Twenty- First Century*, p. 202.

tices, poverty, and ecological destruction. In the Old Testament, prophets make it very vivid that God opposes injustice and hates those who pursue it. As we move towards the coming of our Lord it will become increasingly important that those involved in mission make God's priorities their own, and struggle alongside those with whom they are involved, to show that the Gospel is relevant to the whole life.

III. Secularization

This is also reducing the church attendance and membership. It is a concept relating to a broad process occurring within society. Secularism is an ideology advocating the elimination of religious influence in the state and institutions, particularly in education.[201] This reminds me of a comment we received from the head teacher when we visited a certain school on 22nd of September, 2000, in Ogdensburg in Northern New York when we introduced ourselves as Christians who came to visit a Presbyterian Church in USA.[202] As Christians we expected to open every meeting wherever we went with a prayer. When we arrived at this school after giving and introduction in the office before the official meeting with children, the head teacher warned, "do not mention anything that you are Christians because that might mean that you have come to share your faith". One day a BBC News announcer said openly on the radio in 2002 when he held interviews with a Muslim and a Christian on BBC Scotland. He said and I quote "Scotland is not a religious country. We do not want to be a religious country. Scotland is a secularized country. Those who are fighting in Israel and Palestine fight in the name of Religion. We do not want to be a religious country because Religions fight."[203] An Australian Church leader (Moderator of Presbyterian Church in Australia) came to visit Zomba Theological College in 2003 on the capacity as a moderator as well as our fellow lecturer. During discussion he said "the Church in Malawi is growing tremendously while in my home

---

[201] D.S. Mwakanandi, Missiology: TEEM Notes, p. 49.
[202] USA is one of the countries in which secularisation has reduced Christianity drastically. No wonder my experience during the visit to the Presbyterian Church in Northern New York in September 2000 can tell.
[203] My one year stay in Glasgow has exposed me to many things not only in class but also in other social and religious aspects. Many people including the Europeans themselves do accept that Christianity in Europe (in this case United Kingdom) is not the same as it used to be when missionaries came to preach to other parts of the world like Africa.

country Australia, most people have in time to think of going to church or any meeting to talk and share about God."²⁰⁴ This gives us evidence that secularization is not uncommon. Even in developing countries like Malawi, this is becoming common. Thus when we talk of secularization we mean, that most people feel unwilling to worship God. Their spiritual anxiety has been taken up by worldly events. They have no place for God in their life. They believe and trust in what they possess. Their individualistic philosophy controls their life. Materialism, posh and fashionable life is the centre of their whole being. Unfortunately such people may also see no difference between what is sacred and not. As missionaries to the whole world, we cannot stop preaching and teaching the Living Word who is Christ. Our approach and strategy will not be the same as those who preached and taught three to four hundreds of years ago. Definitely such approach has to take into consideration new methods. For instance the Web Materials should be full of Christian material. The programmes on television must be full of religious teaching material to catch peoples attention to know God. More theological faculties have to be introduced or expanded in the Universities.

IV. Globalisation

Globalisation is a new word formulated from the word global meaning worldwide. It implies something which has affected the whole world or to be more precise everyone. This is not impossible to happen. With high technology, facilities like aeroplanes, computers, television, access to the web and electronic mail and many others, information disseminates so easily. A large number of people are becoming obsessed with these facilities. On a positive note, we should congratulate this development - for this has made many things being done fast and cheap. There is a wonderful network in communication among people and organizations. The world has become really small. However missionary concerns have to point out that this technology carries with it many hazardous effects on the life of a person. For instance, access to some information on the Web is dangerous to the spiritual life of a person. This has spoiled the life of many in the western world, especially the youth, and the gospel is not relevant to them. Too much obsession has

---

[204] Equally in Australia the influence of the church and religion is disappearing from modern societies.

resulted in reducing the personal contacts of people-no fellowship. It has promoted an individualistic philosophy.

But we cannot stop doing our missionary work. What is required is a relevant approach to mission. Probably in this case mission has also to be globalized. Everyone worldwide should take part, should know the technology of today so that he/she is not isolated or disassociated from the present world. As Thompson puts it globalization "indicates the movement towards a real and joyful acceptance of the fact that no one nation or culture or race can claim to represent or have predominance in the Church. It gives reality to the theological truth that people shall come from the east and west, from the north and south, and take their places at the feast in the Kingdom." Therefore taking the meaning of globalization from another perspective, it symbolizes that one day all the people will come together.

"In practice", Thompson adds, "globalization means giving others their proper place in mission: accepting humbly that our part is only a small one; being willing to work with other people, and not simply for them listening intently for the word of the Lord from lips of Africa, Asia and Latin America."[205] It is not surprising that Thomson's missionary interest it geared towards third world countries (Africa, Asia, Latin America) not because his country (Ireland) is already Christianized but probably because the Presbyterian Church in Ireland contributes a lot to the mission work. But this strategy should be highly regarded as it applies to every place.

VI. Contextualization/Inculturation.

Having seen the issues of other religions, increase in ecological/environmental degradation, secularisation, globalization, it would be also important to look at another important area Christians must re-think with seriousness as they carry out missionary work to people of different cultural background. This is the whole area of inculturation and contextualization.[206] These two terms are interwoven and often used interchangeably.

It is pleasing to note that some modern missionaries who come to Africa can say without hesitation that their first brothers who came to evangelize Africa presumed that their culture was superior to African culture. Jack Thompson has this to say "For most of the last one hundred and fifty years

---

[205] Jack Thompson, *Mission in the Twenty-first Century*, p. 208.
[206] D.S. Mwakanandi, *Missiology: TEEM Notes*, p. 53.

missions from Britain and Ireland have presumed the cultural superiority of the society from which they came over that of the society to which they went."[207] Thompson very much agrees hat western missionaries undervalued the cultural and religious heritage of those among whom they were called to serve. [208]

Therefore Thompson is one of the chief advocates of contextualization and inculturation. The chief aim of contextualization/inculturation is to win people to Christ[209] in their own life context, and culture. But Mwakanandi warns against imbalances taking place when doing contextualization which may lead to losing the core message of the Gospel. He says "the concept purports to remove any obvious obstacle in communication. Contextualization aims at confronting people with the gospel and letting them hear God in Jesus Christ addressing them in their own life context. and culture." Thompson also has this to say, "the importance of inculturation and contextualization is that the gospel becomes truly incarnated into the societies in which it is taking root".[210] With contextualization, the Gospel is not received as foreign and subsequently will not fail to get its roots into the ground. It is important that in all aspects, (liturgical, theological, pastoral and ethical) the approach must be in the soil of the people you have come to evangelize.[211]

Some important hints on contextualization in Missions

"Missiology as a critical reflection of Christians engaged in missionary practice in the light of God's Word",[212] can not leave out the issue of contextualization. It is vitally significant to look at 'the Word of God' not only as a source of theology but also as the source of good and viable contextualization.

When discussing missiology in relation to other theological disciplines we noted that missiology and theology are inseparable. We cannot do theology without thinking about its missiological implication. Real theology is that which aims at fulfilling the salvation commission to the world. John Macquarrie has defined theology as "the study which through participation in

---

[207] Jack Thompson, *Missions into the Twenty-first Century*, p. 203.
[208] Jack Thompson, *Missions into the Twenty- first Century*, p. 203.
[209] Mwakanandi, *Missiology, TEEM Notes*, p. 54.
[210] Jack Thompson, *Missions into the Twenty-first Century*, p. 203.
[211] Jack Thompson, *Mission into the Twenty-first Century*, p. 203.
[212] Samuel Escobar, *A Time for Mission*, Inter Varsity Press, Leicester, 2003, p. 20.

reflection upon a religious faith, seeks to express the content of this faith in the clearest and most coherent language".[213] In 'participating in' and 'reflecting upon' a person is actually involved in theology. Therefore while faith is the central component of making theology, faith should be understood through seeking. Theology must relate God to humanity and people should understand God.

But probably the question of where does a missiologist start is crucial at this point. It has been discussed by numerous scholars as to whether a theologian, when doing theology of context should begin from human experience or from God or scriptures. Each approach points in its favour.

"Christian faith" Turner says, "has to be communicated to different categories of people, men/women, literate/illiterate, young/old, poor/rich."[214]

In contextual theology, a constructive role of reason should be articulated and should be formulated. It should however be noted that there is not only one and simple method of doing theology. Rather the method of study is a complex one and several methods are employed. For instance Rudolf Bultmann used demythologization as a tool to attract modern man to the faith (and failed in the attempt), while Karl Barth opted for dialectic theology. He did not write his theology for missions, but missiology can make good use of it.

Missiologists are probably little concerned with either of these two approaches, and they would rather be concerned about how the gospel, which is the whole biblical truth can, reach and be received by people of different backgrounds. True missiologists believe that the basis and foundation of all missionary endeavours is the God's Revelation. Christian religion bases its truth claim on what has happened in human history. It is here that a missiologists can go primarily to seek the source of theology. As Turner correctly argues, "Theology follows from what has been revealed and becomes part of a theologian",[215] even contextualization which is a small component in theology depends on what is given and is then to be applied to the situation. When I mention about revelation, I am more interested in what O' Collins calls '*I -thou*' relationship. While I do not disregard or underrate

---

[213] John Macquarrie, *Principles of Christian Theology*, Charles Scribner's Sons, New York, 1966, p. 1.
[214] T.M. Turner, *Introducing Theology*, Great Britain, 1991, p. 18.
[215] Turner, *Introducing Theology*, p 18.

propositional revelation, and of course, with much respect I know that special and propositional revelations are complimentary, and propositional revelation is in fact the basis of natural theology and also the true knowledge of God, but since it is not complete, I would rather strict myself to the special or I- thou relationship revelation which is experiential, although God still retains his hiddenness.[216] Thus Missionaries or preachers share what they have received and experienced from the Lord through revelation.

This Revelation is found nowhere else, but in the Bible. In this Bible the central figure is Jesus Christ. Karl Barth says that man/ woman is not able to know God except through Christ. Jesus Christ is the bearer of God's revelation.[217] On the same note John Calvin says, "It was impossible for man to ascend to God because he was totally depraved".[218] While some non-Calvinists do not believe in the total depravity of human beings, the truth remains the same to those who believe in original sin and that Christ came because man on his own was not able to approach God sinful. Jesus Christ, the sinless mediator, is therefore the absolute and final self-giving of God for salvation of humanity. A true Christian must claim that Christianity is the absolute religion which has to be preached to every nation and every race. Instead of preaching "outside the church there is no salvation as once said by Cyprian, a missiologist should say "outside Christ there is no salvation because those who have not studied ecclesiology often confuse 'the church' with a denomination. Therefore no true and good theology outside Christ. There might be some people outside of Christianity who may be saved but that is totally dependent on God's grace. We should thus start from the word of God as a testimony to the revelation of God that becomes a representation of the original disclosure to each generation by the inspiration of the Holy Spirit who enables it to be the word of God.

While the Bible is the main source of theology, missiology and mission, it should be mentioned and seriously noted by missiologists that it has faced enormous challenges. It has been questioned as regards to its authority and interpretation. Of course, one may accept that "the Bible in its literal sense is ambiguous. It can be a force for oppression as well as a force for libera-

---

[216] Turner, *Introducing Theology*, p 19.
[217] Karl Barth, *Church Dogmatics*, Westminster Knox Press, Louisville, 1994, pp. 92-110.
[218] John Calvin, in *The New Theological Dictionary* edited by Sinclair B. Ferguson, David Wright, J.I Packer, Inter Varsity Press, Leicester, 1988, p. 122.

tion."²¹⁹ If it is treated like a finished monument that can not be touched then it can be oppressive. Innumerable preachers and theologians have read the Bible literal and have ended up using it as a weapon for oppression. Thus right interpretation of the Bible is the source of relevant theology in doing missiology and mission. The foremost thing in missiology is taking scriptures in their relevant interpretation to the contemporary situation.

Missiologists should translate their faith in terms of their day. But, here also we need to qualify how best this should be done. For example, while a translator when doing his work learns also from the dialogue with the world of his day, he/she does not look to the modern world to find what to do to the situation, rather he/she looks at what the Bible says to such a situation. In this case a rationale is applied but the Bible is central. Our faith needs to be critically analyzed so as to make it intelligible and consistent. Christian faith should give meaning to the people. We noted in one of the preceding paragraphs that missiology is a critical reflection of Christians engaged in missionary practice in the light of God's Word. In almost the same line Pannenberg contends "whatever claims Christians have made must be subject to rationale". This rationale must be analyzed by scripture. Its not only the Christian faith that has to be questioned, but also cultural practices or any theologies that are being made nowadays. One may also be compelled therefore to add to Pannenberg's quotation by saying "whatever claim a person might make to defending his cultural practices that it contains spirituality in it, it still must be subject to question if such spiritual practices are divine or diabolic.

While revelation from Scripture must be used in contextualization a balance must be maintained between what is the revealed truth and what is in the cultural or social setting. Just to explain a bit further, before Christianity came, Malawians knew God. Names of God included Chauta, Chiuta, Chisumphi, Namalenga, Mulungu, etc. While it is true that Africans knew God, probably what should be the task of a missiologist is to find out the concept of God in Africa. Is it the same with that God of revealed in Jesus Christ? It has been reported by some Malawian theologians like Rev Dr Kawale²²⁰ that during his doctoral research it came to his awareness that the name Chauta

---

[219] Helen R Graham, "A Solomonic Model of Peace" in S.R. Surgirtharajah (ed), *Voices from the Margin*, Maryknoll: Orbis, 1991, pp. 220-221.
[220] Dr Kawale was being interviewed on Television Malawi 2003.

originally meant a goddess. Rev Dr Silas Nyirenda[221] has pointed out that one of the negative factors of African Traditional Religions is superstition and the deformation of God so that Africans have beliefs which have no real basis. He also argued that in such a situation God's unique role has been usurped by medicine persons, spirits and superstitious objects. Also on the same note a majority of African theologians like John Mbiti, believe that ancestral veneration is very central in African Traditional Religion.

If that is true then the question would be "is this God the same God that was revealed in Jesus Christ. Are African Traditionalists not practising polytheism? As the Chewa saying goes *"kuona maso ankhono nkhudekha,"* meaning if you want to find the truth about something do not hurry in making conclusions. Thus, this requires a good and thorough research. Those bringing Christianity to such people should not just come and condemn them but rather introduce their Living God with keen interest also to study the people they serve. Things like love, concern and dialogue are important here. Probably this is what early missionaries in the 19th century lacked. Instead of helping Malawians to understand their God better through this new and true religion, they discouraged most of the African cultural practices and customs as pagan not knowing that they had some religious values which were to be studied first and see a point of entry with their Gospel. This resulted in syncretism.

Of course some African theologians like John Mbiti would argue that ancestors are mainly venerated as intermediaries in a similar sense as Jesus is to God the Father. How many African traditionalists would accept that they do not worship ancestral spirits as Mbiti is putting it? This is very polemical. Our concern in this subject is that people's revelation of God is to be closely and critically observed in the light of the scripture. In the process and exercise of contextualization, missiologists are challenged with the task of doing relevant theology and missionary work so that at the end of the day people will embrace the true faith in the true God. This takes us to the next topic on mission and contextualization.

---

[221] Dr Nyirenda's paper on *Africa Traditional Religions on HIV/AIDS and Stigmatization* held in South Africa 4th-8th November 2003, p. 2.

b. Mission and Contextualization.

Bruce Nichols defines contextualization as the translation of the unchanging content of the Gospel of the Kingdom into the a verbal form meaningful to the peoples in different cultures and within their particular existential situation.[222] In this case contextualization actually means to discover the legitimate implications of the Gospel in a given situation, whether cultural, social, economic, political.

Some evangelicals have approached contextualization with a negative attitude in the sense that they always want to give the gospel to people of other cultures without considering their political, social, economic and cultural situations. To them this is one way of maintaining the biblical authority. This also has been common in conservative churches. This is not fair. Hesselgrave reports that the reaction to evangelicals by some contextual theologians like Conn is too critical. Conn is convinced that the Evangelicals' approach to contextualization throws away the baby with the bath water.[223] His work is appreciated especially that he does not leave them unguided. He took the risk of encouraging them to wrestle with the relationship between the biblical text and people's cultural context.[224]

Theologians must allow scripture to judge their own inculturated interpretation and life styles. For Conn, contextualization is the process of conscientizing of the whole people of God to the hermeneutical claims of the Gospel.[225] While contextualization stresses local and situational concerns, it draws its basic power from the gospel which is for all people.

As a plea to theologians, it is important when bringing the gospel one has also to look into the cultural setting of the people. For the good news brought to people to be more effective, it would not be right to abuse the cultural practices in the first instance. But it is rather better to appreciate the different culture you have found. Have time to learn from them, see whether it has certain practices compatible or incompatible with the gospel. John Mbiti, the most popular African theologian states that because missionaries neglected African culture when christianizing Africa, Christianity must begin all over again with the aim of developing a theology for Africans.

---

[222] David Hesselgrave, *Contextualisation*, Inter Varsity Press, Leicester, p. 37.
[223] David Hesselgrave, *Contextualization*, Inter Varsity Press, Leicester, p. 40.
[224] David Hesselgrave, *Contextualization*, Inter Varsity Press, Leicester, p. 39.
[225] David Hesselgrave, *Contextualization*, Inter Varsity Press, Leicester, p. 38.

Although it is true that Africans suffer from a religious *schizophrenia*[226] because of the struggle between their Christianity and their Africanness as stated by Bishop Desmond Tutu, the deficiency which is worthy of criticism in Mbiti's argument is that a new Christianity apart from the present cannot be founded.

It is important to remind ourselves, God already brought his full revelation in Christ once and for all. Perhaps the best approach should be to reform the same Christianity. This reformation can only be done by encouraging African theologians to do contextual theology. In a few years from now it will make a difference. It is already evident that the rise of African theologies has made a big difference in Africa Christianity not because we are starting all over again but rather correcting the mistakes that were made by early missionaries. In doing this, of course, African culture is taken into account in formulating a relevant theology in Africa.

Contextualisation should include indigenization, inculturation, adaptation. All these however will be done in the light of Scripture. In one of his articles Bishop Kalilombe has shown that it is necessary for a theologian to come down to the level of the people they are approaching with the word of God. For literate and illiterate people the approaches cannot be the same.[227] You need to go with the word of God to their respective level without changing meaning and essence of the message.[228]

African Theologians therefore must take the authority of scripture seriously and apply sound hermeneutical principles which will constitute the foundation for a defensible Christian theology.[229] Sound hermeneutical principles take the Word of God seriously, share what God said and is still saying through the Scriptures, open men's eyes to the application of the Word to everyday life, Guided by the Holy Spirit and theologians will have a

---

[226] John Parrat, *A Reader in African Christian Theology*, SPCK, London, Great Britain, 1987.
[227] P.A. Kalilombe, *The Bible and Non-literate Communities* in R.S. Surgirtharajah (ed), *Voices from the Margin*, Maryknoll Orbis Books, New York, pp. 399-400.
[228] John Parrat, *A Reader in African Christian Theology*, SPCK, London, p. 3.
[229] John Parrat, *A Reader in African Christian Theology*, SPCK, London, p. 4.

message for a cross section of people, men/women, old/young, rich/poor, black/white of the present world. Hermeneutical principles which should deal with real African issues must be applied here.

Chapter 10

Contextualizing a congregation in Malawi

Although Malawi has been widely evangelized, there is still need of contextual evangelization of today's Christian church. Almost everyone will agree that culture is not static, it changes and grows with and through time. Truly, so many things have occurred since Christianity was introduced into Malawi. So contextual theology has to take into account: the spirit and message of the Gospel; tradition of the Christian people; the culture in which one is theologizing and social change in that culture.[230] We also see that contextualization itself is not static. It is a dynamic process of the church's reflection in obedience to Christ and his mission in the world, on the interaction of the text as the word of God and the context as a specific of the human condition.[231] Thus contextualization is essentially a missiological concept. It is very proper that the present church should do missions relevant to today.

Before coming to areas and methods of Contextualizing a congregation, it would be important to very briefly mention the behaviour of early missionaries to Malawi. That early western missionaries regarded their culture as superior compared to traditional African culture can not be denied and many modern African theologians have enormously discussed this subject. Their Christianity was carried in a western colonial baggage.[232] But we want to look at their leadership. It has been noted with concern that the missionaries' attitude and practice were discriminatory[233] in the sense that Africans were not taking part in most decision making meetings. One evidence is noticed from what McIntosh reports about Robert Laws, a Scottish Missionary who used to call Malawians as 'his own black boys'.[234] While most Malawians helped in translating the gospel into the local languages and make their own

---

[230] S.B. Bevans, *Models of Contextual Theology*, Maryknoll: Orbis Books, 1992, p. 1.
[231] Sinclair B. Ferguson and David F. Wright (editors), *New Dictionary of Theology*, Inter Varsity Press, Leicester, 1988.
[232] John Parrat, *A Reader in African Christian Theology*, SPCK, Great Britain, 1987,.
[233] Kalilombe in Appiah-Kubi and Sergio (editors), *African Theology en Route*, Maryknoll, 1977, p. 38.
[234] McIntosh, H., *Robert Laws, Servant of Central Africa*, Handsel Press, 1993, 36.

African songs[235] it took some time to fully recognize and acknowledge their services in the missionary work. The probation for ministers took not less than eight years before ordination.[236] Bishop Kalilombe also reports that the same applied to Roman Catholic and Anglican Churches. While in the Presbyterian Church it took about fifty years (1875-1925) to leave missionary work to be done by Africans themselves, it took about seventy-five years (1902-1977) for Roman Catholic Missionaries to consider things from an African point of view.[237] Even after Africans started to participate in missionary work as co-workers with whites, there was still a clear gulf between white clergy and local leaders. Kalilombe also observed that, "in all aspects of church life more importance was put on obedience and conformity to the regimentation and authority from above than on principles of participation, dialogue or freedom of expression."[238]

In light of this background one can correctly say that although many Malawians positively acknowledge and appreciate the gospel received from missionaries, their leadership has often been questioned. Should the churches in Malawi perpetuate this system of leadership? What do parishioners learn from this? What should be the true missionary church today?

Doing Mission of Context Starting with Leadership.

Today we no longer have missionaries and expatriates administering the church. From the time the missionaries handed over the ministry to local people, the church has grown enormously. The church is no longer the same, there are many changes and issues which need serious attention. Although some of the leadership elements have been adopted and inherited from the missionaries, others come as the time and generations change. For example, at present there is more religious diversity than there used to be during the period of the missionaries.

---

[235] McIntosh, *Robert Laws, Servant of Central Africa*, p. 138.
[236] McIntosh, *Robert Laws, Servant of Central Africa*, p. 199.
[237] P.A. Kalilombe *The Presence of the Church in Malawi*, in Torres S and Fabella V.M.M. (editors) *The Emergent Gospel, Theology from the Developing World*, London, Geoffrey Chapman, 1976, pp. 22-30.
[238] P.A. Kalilombe, *The Presence of the Church in Malawi*, in Torres S and Fabella (editors) The Emergent Gospel, pp. 22-30.

While with early missionaries the problem was failure to indigenize, inculturate and contextualize the gospel to the African soil, as they regarded their western culture superior to African culture, the local leaders fail to recognize that other people can perform equally well or sometimes better than they do. It happens that Christian leaders do not want to share responsibilities. Every Christian is invited to the sharing of responsibilities as it is a very vital aspect for church growth. We can be reminded here by what Best argues as the mission of the church. Best is convinced that "the mission of the church is twofold: the gospel to be proclaimed to all nations and the converted are to be taught and observe things for their edification."[239] In the first place the directive 'to all nations' implies that the gospel is not confined to any particular class of people, but open to everyone. Secondly 'teach them' would possibly mean that the continuity and sustainability of Christianity depends on keeping and passing on what has been taught. Christ left the church in the hands of the apostles who passed on the leadership to the present church leaders. Members of the church are as important as leaders like pastors. In fact, members of the congregation are just many parts belonging to one body of Christ (1 Corinthians 12:12-30). Their roles are equally important. If church members realized the talents of each other they would be able to utilize them wisely for the sake of God's Kingdom.

In the Presbyterian Church government, the laity are supposed to be given all leadership roles except those to do with sacraments.[240] Unfortunately some pastors monopolize almost everything leaving little or nothing to be done by lay leaders. Although perhaps the argument would be that the laity do not have theological training, the question is who should train the laity for the congregation. It is wise to invest time in teaching the congregation members the biblical basis for lay ministry. The lay leaders can be empowered if the pastor organizes classes or seminars for them and teach them sermons, pastoral care, leadership qualities and skills so that at least everybody has a task to do.[241] This will keep some members in the church, especially those who feel out of place if they are not given work to do. It is high time that congregations intensified 'on-the-job training'.

---

[239] W.E. Best, "The Church: Her Authority and Mission", WEBBMT, Houston, Texas, 1986.
[240] *The Book of Common Order of the Church of Scotland* revised in 1994, p. 334.
[241] R. Warren, *The Purpose Driven Church*, Grand Rapids, 1995, pp. 309-311.

Kalilombe looking at how congregations operate, has this to say, "the young church today would like to change the system. We need a new set-up whereby the laity will be fully part of the life and work of the church. Probably the hope of new vigor and progress depends on such an overhauling of the system".[242] Therefore building the lay ministry to identify and develop skills empowers them and strengthens church leadership as a whole. Another important thing is that when the church/congregation has strengthened its leadership in knowledge and power it will be the congregation members together taking the initiative in deciding how the gospel needs to be incarnated in their own particular context. They can discuss liturgical, theological, pastoral and even ethical issues[243] which will be relevant to their life context. The old mentality of letting a few individuals run the church must be re-thought and changed.

Probably if church leaders came to the realization that they are put in their positions by God who is loving, caring and faithful they would always be willing to make the church grow for the sake of God's glory.[244] And this growth is mainly dependent on quality missionaries and mission.

Contextualization as a challenge to change among parishioners

Changes in the church will always depend on the context of time and generations. As change takes place, some church members will welcome the changes while others will resist. For instance when the church is dealing with sensitive issues like in times of political crisis, church members have often ended up divided. The dichotomy comes up mainly as to whether the church should be involved in politics or not.[245] Some members would strongly say the church is not authorized to be a political or an economic adviser of civil government. Her mission in the world is to indiscriminately proclaim the gospel of Christ and that social and political problems cannot be solved by the Church.[246] While others would say, as the church preaches Christ it preaches to social beings who have their needs. Therefore it must

---

[242] P.A. Kalilombe, p. 30.
[243] Jack Thompson, *Missions into the Twenty-first Century*, p. 203.
[244] C.C. Mkandawire, *Leadership: A Heart Condition*, Limbe: Assemblies of God, p. 9-10.
[245] During the political transition in 1994 from one party system of government to multiparty system of government the church in Malawi was divided.
[246] Based on the idea of Best on the mission of the Church, in his book *The Church: Her Authority and Mission*, p. 109.

also address social needs of people. In doing so it is automatically involved in politics. Christians are believed to be workers together with God and with one another (1 Corinthians 3:9). So what is the role of co-workers with the Lord? It is the role of church leaders to teach about the role of the church in the society. A general understanding of church teaching on a particular issue by parishioners will reduce confusions in a congregation.

The truth however remains the same, the gospel will never change to please an individual. The role of the gospel is to challenges the existing evils it. In this case as everywhere else, the truth of the gospel needs to take its course. There are reasons why it must do so. Every true church of God studies the situation of the society it serves and makes a theological reflection . The congregation reflects on contemporary life-situations in the light of Christian the faith. "Those doing theological reflection make an attempt to interpret the life experience of their people today in the light of their Christian faith".[247] Theology is done from experience. If the congregation has oppressed and marginalized some members of the church community it will ask itself , what would God have done if he saw these poor and marginalized people? The congregation as the servant of God does what God commissions it to do at that particular time. What will be done here is doing missionary work to your fellow church members.

Almost all African cultural values and are not easily seen as evil. In some Malawian cultures polygamy is part and parcel of life and most Africans argue that it is biblical as it has been reported by Holter.[248] Evangelizing such people would not be easy. Unlike what missionaries did, one has to be considerate and ready to learn why such practices are common and how such can people receive the message of Christ without being offended. To be judgmental and condemn people without knowing and understanding them, does not demonstrate the love and the grace of Christ which he had for all people. A missionary strategy has to be that of compassion and love. Parishioners should not be advised to condemn those who are polygamous. Many people have witnessed polygamists acknowledging their failure before the Lord and have ended up repenting and receive forgiveness. Some have

---

[247] Carlos Abesamis, *Doing Theological Reflection in a Philippine Context*: In Torres Serge and Fabella Virginia (editors), *Emergent Gospel, Theology from the Developing World*, Maryknoll, 1976, p. 112.

[248] N. Shorter, *Yahweh in Africa, Essays on Africa and Old Testament*, Peter Lang, New York, 2000, p. 1.

even send their wives to their homes upon accepting and believing the Gospel and some have decided to faithfully follow Christ, and have abstained going into the house of the second wife who has decided to stay because of children.

The same applies if the church is spiritually dry, and needs revival and new methods of approach to its mission, those in church will seek avenues to achieve the goal, as part of their ministry. The spirit of discernment is there to reveal the mystery of the church ministry. Dulles also argues, "because the mystery of the church is at work, the heart of committed Christians as something they participate, they can assess the adequacy and limits of various models by consulting their own experience."[249] The models here may also refer to the analogies that help to interpret the word of God. Any change or reformation in a congregation be it theological or liturgical has to be handled with care realizing that it will affect everybody in one way or another.

To sum up, the question of why and how a congregation should be contextualized is pertinent. But honestly speaking, it is a complex issue and is almost inexhaustible. It requires pastors, church leaders and all Christians to cooperate. Pope Paul VI said "Adaptation in the field of pastoral, ritual, didactic and spiritual activities is not only possible, it is even favoured by the Church. Liturgical renewal is a living example of this. And in this sense you may and you must have an African Christianity. Indeed you possess human values and characteristic forms of culture which can rise up to perfection so as to find Christianity a true superior fullness and prove to be capable of richness of expression all its own and genuinely African."[250] Malawians should not expect someone from outside to come and improve the church for them. All they need is a sincere effort and commitment to witness and live out the gospel as they contextualize it. All efforts to contextualize and revive the congregation will depend on the leaders and their parishioners. But this also demands understanding and cooperation among people while realizing that it is God doing it through them.

---

[249] A. Dulles, *Models of the Church*, Gill and Macmillan Ltd, Dublin, 1976, p. 25.
[250] Cited by Shorter, *African Theology, Adaptation or Incarnation?* London, Geoffrey Chapman, 1975, p. 20-33.

Chapter 11

Christianity and Islam

The Birth of Islam and Spread of Islam beyond Arabia

The third great monotheistic religion after Judaism and Christianity is Islam. Islam is an Arabic word meaning Submission to the will of Allah. Allah is an Arabic word for God. 'al' the and 'ilah' deity.

The founder of Islam was Abdul Kassim who became known as Muhammad meaning 'the praised one.'[251] He was born in 570 AD in Mecca an ancient city of the present Saudi Arabia. He was an illiterate member of the Quraish[252]- the ruling tribe of Mecca. Orphaned at the age of six he was raised first by his grandfather and then his uncle. At twenty five he married a wealthy widow Khadijah. Some fifteen years his senior, she bore him three sons who died in infancy and four daughters, the youngest of whom and his favourite being Fatima.[253]

When Muhammad was forty years of age in 610, he claimed to have had a vision of the angel Gabriel while meditating in a cave on Mount Hira north of Mecca. Gabriel told Muhammad that he was to be Allah's messenger and promised to dictate to him the word of God the Quran. Many in Mecca strongly opposed Muhammad monotheistic religion as Arabia was polytheistic and his preached against the worship of idols.[254]

In 622 AD, Muhammad fled to Medina 250 miles north of Mecca. This flight is called the Hegira- meaning going forth, a flight which marks year one in Islamic calendar. In Medina Muhammad established himself as a religious and political leader. The city of Medina became the city of the prophet. It is also believed that Muhammad is buried there. Its inhabitants included Christians and Jews who its said undoubtedly influenced Muhammad's thought and theology.

---

[251] John Schwarz, *The Compact Guide to the Christian Faith*, Bethany House, Minneapolis, 1993, p. 183.
[252] Herbert Kane, *A Concise History of the Christian World Mission*, p. 49.
[253] John Schwarz, *The Compact Guide to the Christian Faith*, p. 183.
[254] John Schwarz, p. 183.

In the year 630, Muhammad and his followers fought against and took control of Mecca which became their holy city. Muhammad died in 632 at the age of 61. He did not consider himself to be divine but rather the one chosen by God to be his final prophet-the seal of the prophets. The six prophets of Islam are Noah, Abraham, Moses and Jesus, thus he himself who came after Jesus is claimed to be the lat/final prophet.[255] They also believe in Sin and salvation after death. With this brief background one can easily notice that its beginning is close to Christianity. But there are also several important differences. Some of which are: they believe that Allah is so transcendent and removed while Christians believe that he is transcendent but also immanent and this is possible through Jesus Christ. Muslims do not believe in the Triune God as Christians do as this they think is polytheism. They believe that salvation is by works while Christians believe that Salvation is by the Grace of God. Muslims are not assured of their salvation. They wait until the last day. Christians are assured of their salvation through belief and faith in Christ.[256]

During his life time Muhammad welded an independent, polytheistic, monotheistic people into a united monotheistic nation whose military zeal carried Islam from Arabia Peninsula to the Atlantic Ocean (Morocco) within one hundred years of his death.[257] Wherever Muslims went they fought and imposed their religion on people they found. Perhaps this has been the most common method of the spreading of Islam even up to the present day. If it is not imposed by war it can be imposed through families or marriages or some restrictions to the spread of other religions. It should be intimated here that as we often think of Muslims as Arabs(those who write and speak) we must be aware that the countries with the largest Muslim population nowadays are not Arabic. Indonesia is said to be the largest Muslim country, followed by Pakistan, India, Bangladesh, Turkey, Iran which is Persia, Egypt, Afghanistan, Nigeria and China. Turkey is the largest Islamic country in Europe. Egypt is the only Arabic country in the top ten. It is believed that all these countries became Islam either by conversion or war. But the latter seem to have played a greater role.

---

[255] John Schwarz, p. 183.
[256] John Schwarz, pp. 184-185.
[257] Kane H, *A Concise History of the Christian Mission*, p. 49.

Islam is a faith without priests and sacraments, Muslims worship in Mosques, these are places of prostration which are not churches but buildings where the faithful usually only men, at least in the main hall, gather to pray as a group. The prayers are led by an Imam, meaning he who stand before, a person with religious training who on Friday, Islam's day of formal worship delivers sermon.

Islam's Effect on Christianity.

The warfare with Islam was perhaps far more difficult, dangerous and disastrous to the expansion of Christianity. The followers of Islam embarked on a mission to conquer the whole world. Muhammad the founder as said already in the preceding paragraphs imposed among his followers a unity, hitherto known and inspired them with the sense of mission and not to be afraid to die. Their progress was strongly rapid. They conquered Jerusalem is 638, Caesarea in 640 and as a consequence Palestine and Syria came under Muslim dominion. In 647, Alexandria was captured, Persia in 650, Carthage in 697, Spain in 715, Rome in 846 and Sicily in 902 and the conquest continued.[258]

Egypt, North Africa, Nubia

Christianity spread along the Mediterranean coast of North Africa, taking advantage of the Pax Romana.[259] Finding Greek and Latin already established as languages of trade and army, administration and learning, the Christian messages expressed itself in African soil, through these languages. But Christianity was never simply the religion of the Empire.[260] The witness of the Martyrs in the first century shows that African Christians could stubbornly and courageously resist the civil power. And from Early in its history Christianity in Africa began to be articulated in vernaculars. Coptic language and Coptic culture were introduced in Christian circles. Thus at this time, Christianity experienced what we may call 'tranquillity.'

With the capture of Alexandria and Egypt by the Islamic armies in 640s, Islam spread more rapidly than Christianity in the first 400 years earlier, Islam took over inheritance of the collapse Roman Empire imposing a new

---

[258] D.S. Mwakanandi, *Missiology TEEM Notes*, p. 22.
[259] Kevin Ward, *'Africa,'* in Adrian Hastings (ed.), *A World History of Christianity*, Cassell, London, 1999, p. 193.
[260] Kevin Ward, *'Africa,'* in Adrian Hastings (ed.), *A World History of Christianity*, p. 193.

metropolitan language-Arabic, which replaced Greek and Latin for the Romans and also replaced Christianity the imperial religion.[261]

According to Ken Ward,[262] some of the factors contributing to fall of Christianity are as follows.

I. The unity and moral fervour of pristine Islam in stark contrast to what appeared to be a fractious and worldly Christianity contributed to the success of Islam. And the fact that Christianity in Africa so decisively collapsed in the face of Islam poses difficult historical and theological problem for Christianity in general and African Christianity in particular.

II. Africa Christianity lacked indigenous roots. Not that Christianity had failed to incorporate itself into local culture and Islam succeeded in this, but rather that religions as opposed to local traditional culture were seen as being inextricably bound up with universal civilization. It was almost impossible to disentangle Christianity and civilization. For instance, when in North Africa, the Greco-Roman Civilization was replaced by that of the Arabs this was signified by a change to a new but equally universal monotheistic religion.

III. In the West Christianity failed particularly because of the persecution which took place against the Copts for their adherent to the one nature (monophysite) theology which was condemned at the Council of Chalcedon. The coming of the Arabs provided a refuge for the persecuted Christians who were regarded as heretics by the Roman Catholic Church.

IV. Muslims were more tolerant to the local people than Christianity was.

V. The increasing growth of Muslim rulers who earlier on realized on the Coptic Christians in learning the Coptic culture later decided a strategy that Christian men must not be allowed to marry out of the Muslim community, but Muslim men must marry Christian women and the children would be Muslims. And by 10th century, the Coptic community became a minority

VI. Christians were discouraged to build more churches where they could gather for worship.

VII Islam introduced taxes to Christians. If they did not join Islam they were asked to pay taxes as a punishment for not leaving their religion.

In spite of all these pressures on Christianity, Christianity did not die completely. Coptic Christianity continued to focal point for a wider African

---

[261] Kevin Ward, '*Africa*,' in Adrian Hastings, p. 193.
[262] Kevin Ward, '*Africa*,' in Adrian Hastings, p. 194-186.

Christianity and flourished in the Nile Valley and later spread to southern parts of North Africa.

However it is worth noting with concern that Islam took advantage of Christian church's weaknesses like doctrinal divisions, focus on civilization and materialism and then immoral practices among Christians. The similar situation in Christian church today has contributed to the failure of missionary work. In many places today, the method of the spread of Islam has not changed. Our concern in missiology is that Islam like any other missionary obstacle, stands as a challenge to the missiology. How do we evangelize to Muslims?

Missionary Work to the Muslims

In the first place we should be made to understand that the relationship between Christians and the members of other religions is very important in every society. These people of different religions live together probably as a nation or as a tribe, they may even belong to one family. Above all they are all people of God created in his own image. If anything transpires as a result of misunderstanding in their faiths and beliefs a dialogue[263] would be the best solution. Mistakably because of their different religious background people have not been keen to establish this spirit of dialogue. Dialogue does not really mean to 'yield to' or compromising your faith. It is rather an act of creating an environment where people of different opinion are able to understand each other and live together in harmony, by being tolerant and respectful to each other while each one knows and keeps his/her identity. If there have wars in the world history, many historians will agree with me that religious wars are among the most disastrous ones.[264] But religious wars should not instill fears in people and end up compromising their faith.

Before a Christian decides to evangelise or do Missionary work to or among Muslims, he/she should be aware and strongly convinced that Christianity is not just another missionary religion as other religions are but rather that it is a unique and living religion in its own nature. Its uniqueness and life comes in the way God has revealed himself through it, in history and in scripture. The climax of the revelation of God is the personality of Christ.

---

[263] David A. Kerr, '*Christian- Muslim Relations,*' in Kerr James M. Phillips and Robert T. Coote (eds.) *Toward the 21st Century in Christian Mission*, Grand Rapids, 1993, pp. 348-362.

[264] The reference to Muslim wars to spread their religion, crusades, wars between Israeli and Palestinians are relevant here.

The word became flesh and dwelt among us (John 1:14). This Christ-our Saviour and Messiah and the Son of God - lived and ministered unto people. Christ was unique in his teaching, which has influenced the life of the world through the centuries. He was also unique in his life and character as supremely 'the man for others,[265] with infinite compassion for everyone. After fulfilling his mission he died and rose from the dead. His Death, Resurrection and Ascension are biblical historical facts. He ascended into heaven and sitteth at the right hand of God Almighty. He intercedes for his followers (Heb 4:14-16; 8:26-27) and he will come again to judge the Living and the Dead and is the Lord forever.

There is no man in the history of all the world religions like Jesus, who lived such a perfect life, died and rose again from the dead. He gave his life, authority and power to his followers- the present Christian Church. Thus the Christian church witnesses the Living Christ. It is nothing else but the Christ's Great Commission that compels Christians to go 'into all the world' to share good news about this Saviour who is to come again. There is no any other name given on this earth to save but this name-Jesus of Nazareth.

However it is more challenging if Christian church takes the gospel to a religion that has much in common like Islam than other religions which are very different from Christianity like Hinduism. It is more importantly for this reason that serious and wise approach has to be sought when evangelizing Muslims. The similarities should not persuade Christians to compromise their Faith but should instead be regarded, as Jesus said, as the evidence of the signs of the nearness of the Second Coming of our Lord when false prophets and anti-christs will be prevalent.

I want to suggest some practical approach to the Mission to the Muslims

I. Christians need to know and master their religion well. They must know their Bible to stand for the truth as they witness to Muslims.

II Also they need to study and know Islam as a religion which stands as a competing religion. Study, understand and interpret it well.

III. Look for things which are common to both religions so that they can act as *bridges* between them. By using their false doctrine or their half truth teaching you can point out their weaknesses or flaws and apply your true Christian Teaching.

---

[265] *New Dictionary of Theology*, Ferguson and Wright (editors), Inter Varsity Press, Leicester, 1998, p. 699.

IV. Expose your Christian literature to them as much as you can and even allow them to come to your Christian Institutions.

V. Be prayerful and strong in your faith so that you stand the challenges as you may face opposition and resistance. This will also reduce chances of compromising the gospel.

VI. Where they have decided not to accept your gospel, just be prayerful, tolerant but do not compromise. Even if you face opposition and resistance, you still need to love and respect them

VII. Christians should extent their social services/ responsibilities like charitable works to everybody including the Muslims as beneficiaries.

Chapter 12

Doing mission and fighting HIV/AIDS

If a theologian today can deliberately leave out HIV/AIDS subject in any theological discipline particularly missiology then he/she is terribly out of context. HID/AIDS is the context of the day worldwide. No parish minister will serve in his congregation without being affected by HIV/AIDS issue. This can be either through his parish programme engagements or in his own family. Any mission subject, therefore, must not leave out commenting on the pandemic. Since now it seems less intriguing to tell people about how HIV/AIDS is contracted and spread because many are aware and a great deal has been written on the subject, probably its effects on life compels people to listen better with kin interest. I want to briefly comment on the effect of the Pandemic.

HIV/AIDS scourge is admittedly the most outstanding challenge facing humanity worldwide. To be more precise the pandemic affects almost every individual in one way or another. People worldwide accept that it is an advent quite new in our time, which no doubt demands critical attention of all disciplines, departments, the private sector, government, non-governmental organizations and based faith organization. The virus which causes this disease is spreading at a frightening scale and with devastating effects especially among the world's most vulnerable and marginalized communities. In some countries especially in Africa, it has pervaded all spheres of life, be they social, economic political or cultural.

With this awareness, Kenneth Ross says that "the rapid spread of HIV/AIDS is an issue which we all need to take to heart."[266] It is an issue taken more importantly to the hearts of all Christians. His approach to this pandemic is christocentric. He thinks the best and fundamental question to be asked in this situation would be, What would Jesus do. In light of this question we can say that bringing Christ to people infected and affected with is very essential. But how do we bring Christ to them?. It is not always easy to bring Christ to somebody who has suffered illness for along time. The temptation that comes is to think that God has abandoned that person. Such

---

[266] K.R. Ross, *Following Jesus and Fighting HIV/AIDS*, St Andrews Press, Edinburgh, 2002.

being the case, mission work to such people be it counselling, should be tactful, with prayers led by the Holy Spirit.

As Jesus identified with the poor, sick, and excluded members of the society, we are bound to pay particular attention to all who are affected by the spread of the HIV/AIDS pandemic and, in regard to each, to consider who Jesus is and what it means to follow him.[267] Christ being the head of the church and Christian members being the parts of the body, we cannot run away therefore, from the fact that the Church is there for the sick, the dying, the bereaved, the orphaned, the widowed, offering love and hope in the gospel of Christ.[268] When one part of the body suffers all parts suffer with it and when one part is well all parts rejoice with it.

I will summarize ten points Ross has suggested to be practiced when combating the HIV/AIDS pandemic. I have noted that Ross's points are not just theological but more importantly missionary strategies. His biblical quotations are very relevant to the subject.

I. Providing Practical Care for People Living with HIV/AIDS.

On this subject Ross quotes Mark 1:40-44. This text is about a leper who came to Jesus to seek healing. In Jewish Law starting from the time of Moses, people with leprosy were abandoned and excluded from the rest of society. Not only that, they were also, according to Leviticus 13:45-46, unclean and outcasts. Jesus turns the law upside down.. He does not only welcome him but also heals him so that he is part of society enjoying a full life. Ross asks us "Following our Lord and Saviour, who was filled with compassion and who reached out to touch the sufferer when he was confronted by disease, can we do anything else?"

I think we can do something following our Lord. The task of missionaries is to reach out and touch everybody regardless of status in the society, especially those suffering from poverty, oppression and diseases. Those who are gifted in healing ministry, let them be given the chance to pray for the patients. Those who can provide for physical needs by giving whatever they have would be a blessing and much consolation to the people living with AIDS.

---

[267] K.R. Ross, p. 1.
[268] Part of Dube's quotation cited by Ross, p. 72.

II. Breaking down the Stigma.

The relevant quotation is Luke 7:36-38, 44-47. The sinful woman was stigmatized by society! shunned and despised by respectable people. Jesus showed the woman love and acceptance. Societies react to HIV/AIDS by stigmatization and isolation. But we should be aware that if there is a behaviour which can make the illness worse it is to reject a patient. Anglican Bishop Gideon Byamugisha says "stigma and rejection hurt more than HIV death".

We praise God that to those who are stigmatized in society, Jesus breaks through the stigma and shows love and receives them and he even dines with them. This good act can not be ignored by the missionary church wherever it is. If the church has kept silence, leaving out the shunned and despised it must re-define its missionary theology. Professor Ross even calls all churches to repent of the discrimination against people living with HIV/AIDS.[269]

III. Words of Hope under the Shadow of Death.[270]

Read John 11:21-27. In this chapter we read the story about the death of Lazarus. We can all agree that death, as it puzzled Martha and Mary the sisters of Lazarus, has puzzled all people of the world. Kauta Msiska explains the effect of death, "Death to us is destruction and not only the end of the life of the one who is dead, but also confusion of the whole of the clan or family".[271] As such it is the biggest problem to everyone. It becomes even worse if the death is no frequent like at this time of HIV/AIDS.

When Lazarus died Jesus had to comfort Mary and Martha by raising their deceased brother. This gave hope of life after death. People living with HIV/AIDS need words of hope and encouragement desperately. It becomes so encouraging that some patients with HIV/AIDS can stand up and encourage others suffering from the same disease to have hope beyond death. Christians carry with them the word of God. This word is Christ himself. Sharing the word of Hope with people who are terminally ill is a very important pastoral activity. To those who are desperate and hopeless words

---

[269] K.R. Ross, Following Jesus and Fighting HIV/AIDS, p. 17.
[270] K.R. Ross, Following Jesus and Fighting HIV/AIDS, pp. 21-25.
[271] S.K. Msiska, *Golden Buttons: Christianity and Traditional Religion among the Tumbuka*, CLAIM-Kachere, Blantyre, 1997. p. 51.

of hope are life. JESUS is the way, the truth and the life. Let us take the people with HIV/AIDS to Christ who is all in all. Take time to be with those who are terminally ill. Those who accepted Christ already give them the word of blessed assurance and those who have not accepted Christ as their Saviour, provided the chance before they die.

IV. Caring for Orphans.

Professor Ross reports that HIV/AIDS has created over 13 million orphans of which 95% live in Sub-Sahara Africa. The majority of these children live in situations where resources are scarce. Many are cared for by members of the extended families who stretch their meagre resources. Several grand parents care for 20 or more grand children whose parents have died. Destitute youth fend themselves. Carol Finlay who worked at Ekwendeni for many years has a testimony about Mercy an orphaned student nurse.[272] Carol has often times recited Mercy like this, HIV/AIDS to me means death, orphans, and bereaved parents". In this world of HIV/AIDS where the figure of orphans is increasing enormously, is mandate from God that Christians must realize where their responsibility lies. They should be aware that Christianity is a religion whose teaching is also centred on caring for orphans and widows.

V. Equipping Young People for Life

Read Mark 9:42. This chapter has been used by many churches many times. During baptism or any function that is targeting children, this has been the reference text. Jesus is not justifying the sinlessness of children. Rather he is condemning the practice of despising and abusing children during. Professor Ross reports that "the strength of his condemnation underlines the importance of the care which we take to nurture the young and the vulnerable". It has been reported by a number of epidemiologists that most people who are dying of HIV/AIDS are young people in their 20s and 30s. Which means that the most reliable people are swept away by this pandemic.

HIV/AIDS is preventable disease yet many people are making innocent young ones to be infected. It would be better that these children be saved because they are the future of any society, family, clan, nation, or government. Young people whose future lies in the hands of elderly people need

---

[272] Carol Finlay assisted this girl to get her education in the 1990s.

right education. Wrong teachings and bad customs, beliefs and practices can cause a lot of damage to the youths. I want to agree with Ross, that "the Church should have a special role in equipping people to deal with the epidemic. It is particularly important that clergy and lay leaders are offered appropriate training. The capacity to offer effective education in a group context and individual counselling to those who are directly affected is more urgently needed than anything else". [273] Here negligence is equally harmful as misleading or false teaching. As Jesus said, Christians are requested to prepare good education for their spiritual as well as physical growth (Luke 2:52). There must be good teaching on topics like, the role of God in a person's life, pre-marital education, Christian marriage, sex education and the like.

VI Standing in Solidarity with Churches and Communities. (Mark 12:28-31).

Kenneth Ross starts by saying, "nothing is more fundamental in the gospel than the love imperative.[274] The most important commandment Jesus taught his disciples was that of love, "love one another as I have loved you" (John 15:17). With love anything is possible. The Christian message should be centred on the love of God for all human beings but also on the love for one another.

If there is something that HIV/AIDS patients need, it is love. They are human as everybody else is. But sometimes their being sick has created a gulf that they can be treated as not one of us.

VII. Speaking Truth to Power

One of the contributing factors to the rapid spread of HIV/AIDS in Sub-Saharan Africa is choosing not to honest. Jesus was not afraid to tell people quite bluntly that they had their priorities the wrong way-even if he put himself at risk by doing so. In Luke 14:1-4, Jesus healed the sick person on the Sabbath. He was, as a Jew, quite knowledgeable that Sabbath breaking was a serious offence under the Mosaic Law. But it is interesting and worth learning that "for him, the healing was more important than any overenthusiastic commitment to Sabbath observance".[275] Likewise the church should be hon-

---

[273] K.R. Ross, *Following Jesus and Fighting HIV/AIDS*, p. 35.
[274] K.R. Ross, *Following Jesus and Fighting HIV/AIDS*, p. 39
[275] K.R. Ross, *Following Jesus and Fighting HIV/AIDS*, p. 45.

est about its stand in as far her message is concerned. It should not be dragged by 'the cultural set-up rules' as it endeavours to eradicate this disease. The church should even make traditionalists re-thin their beliefs and traditions for the sake of saving the world from HIV/AIDS pandemic. "As the community responsible to articulate in worship the concerns and the prayers of contemporary society, says Ross, "the church cannot evade its obligation to give AIDS its due place in evangelism, preaching and catechesis."[276] This means speaking openly without fear about subjects often regarded as taboo, such as sexual behaviour, gender discrimination, domestic violence, sex and cultural practices.

VIII. Renewing the Community of Women and Men. (Matthew 15:21-28).[277]

The fact that during this passage's time there was a great distance between men and women cannot be overemphasized. Women were associated with religious uncleanliness and their position in worship was far from being realized. The society was undoubtedly androcentric. Their presence among men was not counted. In this story "one of the great distinctive features of Jesus' life was his close association with women. He spent time with women, he showed understanding of the issues which concerned them and unsurprisingly women found Jesus approachable. It can be noticed that many of the great passages of the Gospel are concerned with women breaking through the taboos of the time to engage directly with Jesus. In and through Jesus the community of women and men is set upon an entirely new basis."[278]

The Jewish life situation is not different from some of the societies in the world. For example some Malawian societies are andocentric like that the Jews, men are decision makers and women are supposed to simply obey. Most of the cultural customs and practices oppress and marginalize women.[279] It should be mentioned that in such kind of societies scriptures can be quoted to justify their practice as reported by Mijoga.[280]

---

[276] K.R. Ross, *Following Jesus and Fighting HIV/AIDS*, p. 45-46.
[277] K.R. Ross, *Following Jesus and Fighting HIV/AIDS*, p. 53-54.
[278] K.R. Ross, *Following Jesus and Fighting HIV/AIDS*, p. 53.
[279] T.P.K. Nyasulu, *Pauline Social Ethics in a Malawian Context: The Study of Galatians 3:26-28 and Colossians 3:18-4:1*, MTh, University of Glasgow, 2002, p. 11.
[280] H.B.P. Mijoga, 'The Bible in Malawi,' in West and Dube (editors), *The Bible in Africa*, Brill, 2000, p. 374.

In this case, as was the case in contextualization/inculturation to make the gospel relevant in these societies some cultural practices which oppress women have to be dealt with. As Musa Dube has said "Prevention of HIV/AIDS is not as easy as abstain and be faithful. Rather, it also about dealing with cultural structures that empower male gender over the female gender in our families, churches and societies."[281]

IX. A Bias towards those Infected by HIV/AIDS

Jesus said to them, "It is not the healthy who need a doctor, but the sick. I have not come to call the righteous, but sinners" (Mark 2:17)

As we might remember, Jesus lived his life in a society where sharp distinction were drawn between the 'good' and the 'bad', the 'righteous' and the 'sinners', the 'healthy' and the 'sick'. It was not uncommon "that the righteous despised those who were too poor to observe all the details of the Jewish law, women whose only way of survival was to sell their bodies to the tax collectors who collaborated with the Roman authorities in their community".[282]

It is in this difficult situation that Jesus stood firm opposing religious leaders who called themselves righteous. He tells them, I come not to call the 'righteous' but the 'sinners'.

The message of Incarnation is commonly summarized as 'God identified himself with humanity in Jesus Christ.' He set his tent among human beings. During his ministry as we have seen, Jesus often identified himself with the poor, the sick and the marginalized. The church likewise has this challenging task of identifying itself with people living with HIV/AIDS.

X. Rethinking our Faith.[283]

The question which Christ asked his disciples at Caesarea Philippi in Mark 8:27-29, Who do you say that I am?, is very important not just for its own sake but purposely for the sake of those who are following Christ. Indeed, to know who your master is, is very important. Who is Jesus to us at this time? If Jesus is the Christ the Son of the Living God, the Saviour of our souls it will not be impossible to claim him as our Master and Saviour even during

---

[281] Cited by Kenneth Ross in *Following Jesus and Fighting HIV/AIDS*, p. 56.
[282] K.R. Ross, *Following Jesus and Fighting HIV/AIDS*, p. 59.
[283] K.R. Ross, *Following Jesus and Fighting HIV/AIDS*, p. 65.

this critical time of the epidemic. Jesus identified himself with the sick, sinners, the oppressed. What about his believers?

The Church has come to the realization that it has kept silence about HIV/AIDS or has the talked about it negatively perhaps because of theological misunderstanding about the epidemic. As a result the people living with HIV/AIDS have suffered stigmatization not only in secular societies but also from religious communities. While it is very true that the deadly disease spreads mostly through immoral behaviour, it should be known that some innocent people have died of the disease.

The message of the church should really change. Let it teach about the love of God for everyone including the one with HIV/AIDS. Followers of Christ are to follow him in truth and love. Christ out of his endless love for his people, decided to suffer and die for them. It is this love and truth that will compel Christian members to serve those suffering with dedication, and they must do this untiringly. It is a crisis which invites the whole membership of the Church. Let us bear one another's burden and fulfill the Greatest and New Law of Christ, "Love one another as I loved you".[284]

To wind up, during missionary task or any evangelistic concern a number of methods can be applied to address the HIV/AIDS issue. For example, there is need for awareness-raising of the pandemic in the life of both church and community. This can be done through formal and informal talks and special services to be arranged by the church during worship. Congregations and other groups can form links with communities affected through establishing communication, exploring ways of supporting and praying for one another. Churches can set aside a day like World AIDS Day, when to focus only on HIV/AIDS. During this time *practical* and financial support can be sought and sent to the affected . Well- to do up communities like partner churches and other international bodies should be generous enough to support places terribly hit by the pandemic.

As an African theologian it is also advisable that those stakeholders in fighting the epidemic must include addressing its accompanying epidemics namely, cultural deficiencies, stigma and social injustices which are enhanced by African cultures and beliefs. Also a theological programme that

---

[284] Based on K.R. Ross, *Following Jesus and Fighting HIV/AIDS*, p. 68.

seeks to integrate HIV/AIDS will be a necessity and in all theological Institutions so that theological students after completion of their course go to the people at the grass-root level well equipped.

Chapter 13

Co-operation/ecumenism and unity in mission.

This is a new phenomenon in as far as denominations are concerned. Taking from diversities in the New Testament, many churches have been created and have witnessed Christ in the way they were taught by their forefathers in the faith. Such churches were and are free to develop their own church pattern taken from the Bible. For example those who joined the Roman Catholic Church followed what the Catholic Church taught. Those who decided to be Reformed, Calvinist, Methodist, Lutheran etc, followed what they were taught in as far as their denomination was concerned.

This trend continued, until the early twentieth century, when churches started noting that there was something which hindered the missionary work and this was nothing other than division. Those church denominations doing their missions separately and individually with rivalries instead of preaching the gospel, preached their denominations - the 'isms' like Roman Catholicism, Protestantism, Methodism, Anglicanism. Each denomination was *'the Church'*. Not only did they treat people of other religions like Muslims as people of other faiths, they treated fellow Christians as belonging to other faiths too. To remedy the situation, ecumenism was born. This refers to the biblical area of the unity of the church in the whole inhabited world (oikomene). In preparations for the joint meetings there were theological discussions among missionaries in which the quest for church unity was featured.

The first international conferences for the advancement of missions took place in London in 1878 and 1888 and in New York in 1900. Many conferences have since followed to focus on ecumenism. However the 1910 Edinburgh meeting seems to have stirred the world zeal of Ecumenism. A World Missionary Conference was held discussing concerns of doctrine, polity and practice. This was regarded as the beginning of the modern Ecumenical Movement. In modern times Ecumenism refers to the movement in many churches which seek the unity of the church through the coming together of the churches in discussion, prayer and communication. The main purpose was to plan the next steps in evangelizing the world. Those involved in the first meeting agreed to use every possible means to remove the scandal of divisions. Besides the cooperation in missions, there developed also cooperation in other fields.

In 1927, the first World Conference on Faith and Order took place in Lausanne - Geneva. 1937, a similar meeting took place. In !948, the World Council of Churches was begun. A meeting that was important in as far as ecumenism is concerned was the meeting at Lima in 1982 when an (incomplete) process of consensus on baptism, Eucharist and ministry were started. The world body which strongly advocates ecumenism is WCC. Its role is to strengthen ecumenism between different churches. Its mission statement revised in 1961 says "WCC is a fellowship of churches which accepts our Lord Jesus Christ as Lord and Saviour according to scripture and therefore seek to fulfill together their common calling to the glory of the one God, Father, Son and Holy Spirit".

While this is a good and encouraging move toward missionary work, there are some churches like the Evangelicals who are not in agreement with the movement. They insist that fellowship is impossible without agreement on the basic truths. These, no doubt, stand as challenges to Ecumenism. Their arguments are based on the following reasons:

I. Theological issue: If different denominations were created because of theological matters how can union with unsolved differences be achieved?

II. Ecclesiastical issue. Some Evangelicals are not ready to be in union with churches that do not share their doctrine of the church.

III. Methodological issue: Since a major reason for founding the ecumenical movement was to overcome the drawbacks of a divided witness there is real pertinence to a pragmatic question raised by evangelicals, how effective is the ecumenical movement in carrying out the task of evangelizing the whole world?

IV. Teleological Issue/the Issue of Ultimate Goal: The evangelicals ask, what is the ultimate goal of the ecumenical movement? Is it again a merger of all denominations into a super church?

Willard Erickson responds to the concerns raised by the Evangelicals who are not in favour of Ecumenism. If all Christians claim to be followers of Christ then his last prayer for the church should be the starting point.

1. We need to realize that the church of Christ is one church, all who are related to the same Saviour and Lord and indeed part of the same spiritual body (1 Corinthians 12:13).

II. The spiritual unity of believers should show itself in goodwill, fellowship and love for one another. We should employ every legitimate way of affirming that we are one with Christians who are organically separated from us. Although some Christians belong to a different of denomination, we still belong to one family by virtue of professing Christ as our Lord and Saviour.

III. Christians of all types should work together whenever possible. If no essential point of doctrine or practice, like infant baptism, is compromised they should join forces. There should be occasions for Christians to lay aside their differences. Cooperation among Christians to give common witness to the world is very important.

IV. It is important to describe in great detail the doctrinal basis and objective of fellowship. Although we can differ in doctrines, the execution of Christ's commission is still the major task of the church

V. We must as Christians guard against any union that would sap the spiritual vitality of the church. For example, if the union will reduce the strength and potentiality of a conservative church from growing then it would not be a nice ideal to force the union.

VI. Christians should not be quick to leave their parent churches or denominations. As long as there is a reasonable possibility of redeeming the denominations, the conservative witness should not be abandoned. For that matter, if the conservatives withdrew from ecumenical circles, their position will not be represented therein.

VII. It is important to make sure that divisions and separations are due to genuine convictions and principles and not to personal conflict or individual ambition. It is a discredit to the cause of Christ where Christians who hold the same beliefs and goals separate.

VIII. Where Christians do disagree, whether as individuals, congregation or denominations, it is essential that they do so in a spirit of love, seeking to correct others and persuade them of the truth, rather than refute or expose them to ridicule. Truth will always be linked to love.

Bibliography

Appiah-Kubi K. and Torres S. (eds.), *African Theology en Route, Papers from the Pan-African Conference of Third World Theologians held in Accra Ghana in 1977*, Maryknoll, New York, 1977.

Avery Dulles S.J., *Models of the Church*, Gill and Macmillan, Dublin, 1976.

Baldwin, J.G., *The Message of Genesis 12-50 from Abraham to Joseph*, Inter Varsity Press, Illinois, 1986.

Best, W.E., *The Church: Her Authority and Mission*, W.E. Best Book Missionary Trust, Houston, Texas, 1986.

Bevans, S.B., *Models of Contextual Theology*, Maryknoll, New York, 1996.

Bowen, R., *So I Send You*, London, SPCK, 1996.

Burnett, D.G., *The Healing of the Nations: The Biblical Basis of the Mission of God*, Paternoster Press, Carlisle, 1986.

Dunn, J.D.G., *Jesus, Paul and the Law: Studies in Mark and Galatians*, Westminster/John Knox Press, Louisville, 1990.

Escobar, Samuel, *A Time For Mission*, David Smith and John Stott (editors), Inter-Varsity Press, Leicester, 2003.

Fiedler, Klaus, *The Story of Faith Missions. From Hudson Taylor to Present Day Africa*, Oxford et al: Regnum, 1994.

Frend, W.H.C., *The Early Church*, SCM Press, London, 1982.

Gonzalez, J.L., *Church History, An Essential Guide*, Abingdon Press, Nashville, 1996.

Hastings, A., *A World History of Christianity*, Cassell, London, 1999,

Holter, N., *Yahweh in Africa: Essays on Africa and the Old Testament*, New York, Peter Lang Publishing, 2000.

Warren, R., *The Purpose Driven Church*, Grand Rapids, 1995.

Kalilombe, P.A., 'A Malawian Example: The Bible and the Non-Literate Communities', in Surgirtharajah (ed.), *Voices from the Margin*, SPCK, London, 1995, pp. 421-435.

Kalilombe P.A., 'The Presence of the Church in Africa', in Torres, S., & Fabella V.M.M (editors), *The Emergent Gospel, Theology from Developing World*, Geoffrey Chapman, London, 1976. pp. 22-30.

Kane, J.H., *A Concise History of the Christian World Mission*, Baker Book House, Grand Rapids, Michigan, 1978.

Kidner, Derek, *Genesis*, Tyndale Old Testament Commentaries, Inter- Varsity Press, Leicester, England, 1967.

McIntosh, Hamish, Robert Laws - A Servant of Africa, Handsel Press Ltd, 1993.

Mkandawire, C.C., *Leadership: A Heart Condition*. Assemblies of God Literature Centre Press, Blantyre, 2002.

Msiska, S.K., *Golden Buttons: Christianity and Traditional Religion among the Tumbuka*, CLAIM-Kachere, Blantyre, 1997.

Mwakanandi, D.S., *Missiology: Theological Education by Extension*, Zomba Theological College, 2000.

Niebuhr, H.R., *Christ and Culture*, Harper and Row Publishers, New York, 1951.

Neill, S., *A History of Christian Mission*, Harmondsworth, Penguin, 1964.

Nyasulu, T.PK., *Church in Society: Pauline Social Ethics in a Malawian Context: A Study of Galatians 3:26-28 and Colossians 3: 18-4:1*. MTh, 2002. University of Glasgow.

Parrat, J., *A Reader in African Christian Theology*, SPCK, London, 1987.

Paas, S., *A Conflict on Authority in the Early African Church: Augustine of Hippo and the Donatists*, Zomba Theological College, 2000.

Pretorius, H.L., Odendaal, A.A., Robinson, P.J., Van der Merwe, G., *Reflecting on Mission in African Context: A Handbook for Missiology*, Pro Christo Publications, Bloemfontein, 1987.

Ross, K.R., *Following Jesus and Fighting HIV/AIDS*, St Andrews Press, Edinburgh, 2002.

Sinclair B. Ferguson, David F. Wright, J.I. Packer (editors), *New Dictionary of Theology*, Inter-Varsity Press, Leicester, England, Downers Grove, Illinois, USA, 1998.

Stott John, *Christian Mission in the Modern World*, Inter Varsity Press, Illinois, 1975.

Schwarz, J., *The Compact Guide to the Christian Faith*, Bethany House Publishers, Minneapolis, 1998.

Verkuyl, J., *Contemporary Missiology: An Introduction*, Wm Eerdmans Publishing Company, Grand Rapids, Michigan, 1978.

Ward, R. (editor), *The Westminster Confession and Catechisms in Modern English*, New Melbourne Press, Australia, 1996.

Weller J., and Linden J., *Mainstream Christianity to 1980 in Malawi, Zambia and Zimbabwe*. Mambo Press, Gweru, 1984.